MW00452829

Pastor/People.

Celestine Briley
20405 Mckonney Hwy
Stony Creek, Va. 23882

"God's People Hurt Me, But His Word Healed Me!"

Ain't No Hurt Like Church Hurt

A Practical Guide for Healing and Moving
Beyond "Church Hurt"

Dr. Vernon D. Shelton, Sr.

Foreword by

Dr. Kevin M. Northam

ISBN: 9781798757840

Developing Disciples Publishing
Amityville, New York 2019

This book is dedicated to "My Adopted Daddy"
Deacon James Gatling (RIH) and all those
Who have been hurt at Church, or by God's People.

Acknowledgements

I would like to take this time to thank my Lord and Savior Jesus Christ who has blessed me with undeserved favor and blessings. I truly understand that it is only by His grace and mercy that I am who I am and have accomplished so many great things in my life and ministry. To God be the glory for the great things He has done!

I am always grateful for my wife, LaPrena, for being my partner in life and ministry. I thank you for your continuous support and the many sacrifices you continue to make so I can fulfill my ministry calling. I would also like to thank God for my children: Terrance, Monique, Myriah, Ayona, DJ, and my grandson, Amari. I am forever grateful for my parents: Marolyn Tucker, Vernon G. Shelton and Lynn Saunders, who have always supported my goals and dreams.

I thank God for my grandmother, Francis Berman, for setting the spiritual foundation of our family. I thank God for my mother and father in-love, Darlene and Michael Moulton. I cannot forget Grandma Jackie who regularly gives spiritual encouragement to all of us. I thank God for all of my siblings (Scooby, Tish, Darrin, Shaquan, Angie, Isha, Sid, Kurt, Charde and Shawniece) as well as my entire family who always support my ministry.

I thank God for my friends for life who are more like brothers, Ronald McNair, Kenny Powell, Demitrius (Man)

Holmes, Ronald Scribner, Greg (Honey) Cunningham, Troy Blackwell, and Corey (Mookie) Tyson.

I thank God for my pastor and father in ministry, Dr. Anthony M. Chandler Sr., for not only pastoring me through one of the toughest seasons of my life, but for setting a great example and developing in me a Spirit of Excellence. Words cannot express the impact you have made upon my life and ministry. I thank God for my mentor and favorite preacher Rev. Jimmy C. Baldwin.

I thank God for my Holy Trinity Baptist Church family; I love you from the bottom of my heart. Thank you for taking care of my family and trusting me to lead you on this journey of faith. This book is dedicated in loving memory of a man who has impacted my life and ministry in a major way prior to going home to be with the Lord. Deacon James Gatling; you will never be forgotten.

I thank God for my editorial staff, Sister Kitty Booker and Jordan Stevenson; your hard work and insight are appreciated. I thank God for the Moderator Gilbert Pickett, the Eastern Baptist Association and my Congress of Christian Education family and staff. I also thank God for the Empire Baptist Missionary Convention and its president, Dr. Carl Washington Jr. In addition, I want to give a special thank you to Dr. James Banks, Dr. Edward O. Williamson and the entire Empire Congress of Christian Education family.

I thank God for my accountability partners and brothers in ministry, Rev. C. Omarr Evans, Dr. Sedgwick Easley, and

Dr. Kevin M. Northam, for your contributions to this book and presence in my life are greatly appreciated.

Thank the Lord for my pastoral friends and colleagues in ministry, Dr. Lemuel Mobley, Rev. Gilbert Pickett, Rev. Evan Gray, Rev. Jeffery S. Thompson, Rev. Patrick Young, Rev. Donald Butler, Rev. Herman Washington, Dr. Robert Young, Dr. Daris Dixon-Clark, Rev. Gary Johnson, Dr. Keith Hayward, Rev. Shaun Jones, Bishop Calvin Rice, Dr. Rodney Coleman, Dr. Leandre Marshall, Dr. Steven Daniels, Bishop Phillip Elliott, Rev. Christopher Howard, Rev. James Furman, Rev. Roger Williams, Rev. MarQuerita Story, Rev. Lawrence Mosley, Dr. Patricia Rickenbacker, Rev. Rodney McFarland, Rev. Stephen Lawrence and Dr. Alonzo Smith. I would be remiss if I did not mention my daughter in ministry, Rev. Robin Turner, one of my greatest supporters.

Lastly, I want to thank every pastor, preacher, lay member, family member and friend who has ever prayed for and pushed me to be a better pastor and person. Thank you for all that you have deposited in my life.

Table of Contents

Foreword

The challenges against today's church are varied in nature, but an increasing exodus of attendees is at the forefront. A new wave of apathy and complacency has set in without a pinpointed single cause. Moreover, a growing vibe called 'church hurt' has been credited as a major reason for the decline among worshippers.

I am not surprised that this book would evolve from one of the greatest young ministry minds and servant leaders of this generation. Dr. Vernon D. Shelton, Sr. has embarked upon a critical subject at a most critical moment in the life and existence of the church. Although he has previously authored practical guides for rebuilding churches and leading churches through change, this presentation is essential for believers at all levels. We all have experienced some form of church hurt.

Dr. Shelton helps to identify the different types of human actions and behavioral patterns that can result in internal conflicts within the church and among her parishioners. As church leaders we are cautioned to be mindful of the nature of humanity, imperfection of the saints and nonproductive attitudes included within most, if not all, congregations. The results of church conflict may lead to individual disappointment, anger, pain and dissention even between the faithful followers of Jesus Christ. The hurt that is created from these emotional, physical and spiritual encounters can become overwhelming to those who are journeying in their faith.

With the publication of Ain't *No Hurt Like "Church Hurt,"* we can analyze the realism that many churches face and carefully consider how some forms of resolution can be implemented. Dr. Shelton has masterfully coupled his years of training along with congregational leadership experience to offer another practical work that would benefit any recipient of church hurt. This book is a timely must read.

Rev. Dr. Kevin M. Northam, Pastor
Olive Branch Baptist Church, Dinwiddie, VA

Praise and Reflection

Life is full of paradoxical moments. We live in an age where we possess bigger houses but smaller families. We have more technology but less time. We spend more money yet seemingly have less. However, as a believer the greatest paradox exists in the place where we seek help and healing is often the place that breaks and hurts us the most. From a very biased point of view, largely because I have dedicated my entire life to the church, I believe the church, although flawed, is still the greatest institution in the world. It has been said there is no hurt like church hurt. Nothing can bruise, or mentally and spiritually drain a person, like experiencing brokenness in the place believed to heal and help.

It is interesting there are times we get mistreated or disrespected in retail stores yet continue to patronize it. We go to work with people who do not appreciate or value our contributions to the company, yet continue to clock in daily. However, in comparison, once a person experiences hurt in the church, they frequently leave and never return, or stay and cause major confusion. Scenarios such as these occur because we fail to understand the same people who come to church on Sunday are the same people we encounter in the community and struggle on so many levels. Once a person is committed to the church, the greater the level of expectation becomes. Regardless of expectation even the most devout Christian makes mistakes at times. One should never be devalued, ostracized or feel pain or hurt because they did not live up to the expectations of others.

Church hurt is real. The effects of church hurt can last a lifetime, and in some instances, possibly have deadly effects. We live in an age where more and more pastors are committing suicide, a great falling away from the church, and everything pertaining to church is magnified. The reason the church is not perfect is because the people it is comprised of are not perfect, we are all a work in progress!

Many times, the church is only viewed from the point of view of the pew. The church is so much bigger than a 90 minute service on Sunday morning. The more involved a person becomes in the life of the church, the greater the chances he or she will encounter moments of unbelievable and undeniable hurt. We can become so bruised in the church simply because, although we confess to sharing the same beliefs and values, there are still varied opinions, ideas, and morals of these believers. So many people who loved the church have walked away, not only because they have been hurt, but often times because their pain has been ignored or even minimized. Whenever a wound is not addressed, it runs the risk of infection which can have a negative impact on the entire body.

The greatest antidote for church hurt is forgiveness. Although the church preaches forgiveness, unfortunately, it is not always practiced. Forgiveness is not just for the one who has been offended but also for the offender. The longer we hold on to hurts and issues with no resolve it creates an atmosphere which is the antithesis of what we confess. The scripture says in Matthew 6:12 "...and forgive us our sins, as we have forgiven those who sin against us." The more we practice forgiveness the greater our ability becomes to handle hurt on any level.

I am convinced more than ever before that the saying hurt people, hurt people is true. In a number of instances, those who inflict hurt on others are dealing with internal issues themselves. I read recently on a social media post that if we do not address our own hurts we will end up bleeding on people who have not cut us. Beyond forgiveness, the church also needs to become a resource center where referrals can be made to counselors, therapist, psychologist and other professionals for holistic care. Pastors and leaders have to be intentional to reassure members there is nothing wrong with seeking professional help. There may be needs beyond the abilities a particular church is able to handle. So often we address the symptoms of hurt and never really identify or deal with the root cause.

Furthermore, it is important to have a realistic view of the church. One thing we do not address often enough is what I call "*Hierarchical Hurt*". This is when officers and ministry leaders use their power, position and influence to hurt, bully, or negatively influence others for their own purposes or gains. Church leaders, including pastors, are there to assist in carrying out the Great Commission--not scatter the flock.

Each individual who attends church has a different level of tolerance, patience, and strength. The way we interact with one member may not be the best way to interact with another. We must value the individuality and uniqueness of all.

In this book, Dr. Vernon Shelton has given us a bird's eye view and stretched our minds about church hurt. His practical insight is helpful for any context. Dr. Shelton's synergy of intellect and practical ideas will stretch the minds of those who are still committed to not only work in the church but ultimately be the church. This work pushes us beyond our pain and challenges us to focus on purpose.

Finally, there have been times I have listened to the meteorologist about the forecast only to find they had it totally wrong; but I still listen to weather reports. There have been times I have received advice from those I admired and respected but realized their point of view was incorrect; but I still value their opinion. I have ordered food at the drive thru only to get home and realize something was missing from the order; but I still go to Chic-fil-a. And so it is with the church, although flawed in many ways, I still believe in the power of God and His church. As hymnologist penned *"It has landed many a thousand."*

Rev. Dr. Sedgwick V. Easley, Pastor
Union Baptist Church, Hempstead, New York

Endorsements

"The church is supposed to be a place of healing and comfort. But how do you deal with pain coming from a place that's supposed to heal. Church hurt is real, but it occurs on so many levels. It can affect anyone from people to pastor, from laity to leadership. Dr. Shelton takes a 360º look at the hurt that takes place. Understanding different perspectives may lead us all on a positive path of healing." – **Rev. C. Omarr Evans, Pastor of Community Baptist Church, Bayside, NY.**

"In this powerful and provocative book, Dr. Vernon Shelton, Sr. explores more deeply the often shallowed historical explorations to unpack this thing we know as "church hurt." While using both personal and communal experiences, Shelton encourages the reader to unpack their own church hurt, while also challenging the reader to seek God and trust God for   priceless revelations that will strengthen the relationship between them and God even though they've experienced church hurt..."- **Dr. Rodney L. Coleman, Sr. Pastor of First Baptist Church of Chapel Hill, Chapel Hill, NC.**

It has been said that there is no hurt like church hurt. Throughout the existence of the church, countless individuals have experienced first-hand hurt, betrayal, and mistreatment in a place that is supposed to be a place of love, hope, healing and wholeness. This reality can leave some reluctant to re-engage, afraid of being hurt again, wanting to protect themselves, and questioning the place of church in their lives. The reason church hurt exist in the first place is because the church is full of imperfect and hurt people who have not adequately dealt with their own past hurt. Thus the old adage hurt people hurt people.

Pastor Shelton provides us with a prescriptive plan for moving past the pain that so often prohibits our progress. A plan for overcoming our past church hurt that relies upon the Word of God. A plan that begins relying upon the power of God to forgive those who have been the purveyors of our pain. A plan that proclaims loudly that in the end love will eventually prevail. – **Rev. Jeffery S. Thompson, Pastor of Amity Baptist Church, Jamaica, NY.**

Introduction

I Can't Believe it Happened at Church

Introduction

I Can't Believe it Happened at Church

HAVE YOU EVER BEEN HURT? Have you ever been hurt by someone you loved? Have you ever been hurt by someone you thought loved and would take care of you? I believe everyone reading this book has experienced some type of hurt, whether it be via family, friends, romantic relationships, places of employment or even life itself. The majority of people have experienced some form of disappointment, betrayal and let down in their lifetime. If you have never been hurt or betrayed, do not be too quick to celebrate. If you just keep living, you will inevitably experience hurt on some level; it's an inescapable reality.

The reason I say everyone will experience some form of hurt or betrayal stems from the fact that life is full of disappointments. Life does not always go according to plan. People do not always do the right thing; nor do things always work out the way we plan. For instance, you can raise your child in church, send him or her to the best private school, teach him or her right from wrong and provide everything needed to have a good life. Nevertheless, he or she may still grow up and do some things they know are not right. You can give your all in a relationship hoping for the best, only to end up disappointed and wishing you would never have wasted your time. The bottom line is, life does not always go according to plan and sometimes it leaves people hurt and wondering what happened.

This is also true for Christian believers. Being a Christian and faithfully attending church does not exempt you from life's realities. You can be a faithful church member, perhaps even possess a title or an important position within the church, and still get hurt. Regardless of who you are in the world or in the church, you will face some type of disappointment and have to deal with hurtful situations. People will let you down. Friends will betray your trust, and even the people you love will disappoint you. No one, and I mean no one, is exempt from life's disappointments. Good situations will go bad. The Bible says in Matthew 5:45, the rain will fall on the just as well as the unjust. Everyone will go endure at least one hurtful event in this thing called life, even God-fearing Christians.

Now, let me push this a little further. Although some Christians do not like to admit it, we will not only get hurt by people in the world. More than likely, all of us will get hurt by people in the church at one point or another. Let's face it, a building may have a cross hanging in the sanctuary and be filled with people professing to be children of God; yet, this does not mean everyone will be treated with love. In the same way people are mistreated in the world, they can also experience it in the church. Here's why: the majority of the people you see at the malls, on your job, or in your neighborhood are the same people who attend churches every Sunday. If people are mean and nasty in the streets, at work, or at home, they more than likely will bring that same spirit in to church.

Throughout my life, I have learned a person may claim to know Jesus, but that does not mean they truly follow Him. Church clothes do not change a person's character. The ability to quote scriptures does not guarantee a person will treat people with respect or love. People do not develop a Christ-like character simply because they can quote scriptures. They develop a Christ-like character when they live by the scriptures. Attending church regularly does not guarantee they are abiding by the scriptures. Sadly, there are often a number of people in church not being changed by the church. Some of the same people or issues you encounter in the world will also find you in church.

One aspect people should keep in mind is the church is not perfect. The primary reason is because it is full of imperfect people. Take for example; say you somehow believe you have found a perfect church. Like it or not, all of that changed the minute you showed up simply because you are

25

not perfect. The Bible is clear, "All have sinned and fall short of the glory of God" (Romans 3:23). Everyone in church has a past and everyone has done something wrong before they were saved and yes, even after they get saved. Christian or non-Christian, we all have stepped outside of the will of God at one time or another. There are no perfect churches as long as they have people inside of them.

I remember when I was a child my grandmother told me I should never put people on a pedestal. Likewise, be mindful that everyone in church is human and will make mistakes and bad decisions. The church is full of sinners who have been saved by grace. This conversation was brought on one Sunday after church when I came home devastated and with a concerned look on my face. The reason being looking I overheard a church mother use vulgarity in the kitchen while talking about the pastor. When I heard what the mother of the church, a respected member, say those things about the pastor, I was stunned and somewhat distraught. As a child, I thought all people who went to church were true Christians, not mere "church folks." I never knew church folks used bad language until I overheard that conversation take place in the kitchen. After that, I did not know what to think about church folks.

My grandmother advised me to stay focused and not allow what I heard to discourage my relationship with God. She wanted me to understand that people in church are not perfect. Little did I know, she was preparing me for the future and helping me understand that church folks are not without fault. In fact, despite being saved, in many cases they still have things to work on. This is one of the reasons I believe so many people get disappointed in church; they somehow have forgotten God's people are not perfect. We all make mistakes and bad decisions. Yet, for some reason, people think because a person is a Christian or a member of a church they will automatically do all the right things. Unfortunately, this is not the case. All Christians and frequent churchgoers fall short and exemplify carnal behaviors at times. The church is not exempt from negative, hurtful and ungodly things happening within the walls of the houses of worship.

Yet in still, I love going to church. I love worship and being in the presence of other believers. However, I realize that we are still people and none of us are have attained the level we need to be spiritually. While we may be saved, we have not been fully delivered from all of our carnal ways. With that in mind, even in church, we still have to deal with jealousy, gossip, backbiting, malice, attitudes, betrayal and many more traits that are not Christ-like.

If for some reason you think this is an exaggeration and none of this takes place within the house of God, all you have to do is become involved. You will discover some church folk are a "trip." Let me be transparent for a moment. When I was a child, I enjoyed everything about church. The trips during the summer, the Easter and Christmas plays, going to Sunday school, children's church and all the fun activities that came along with youth ministry. When I was a child, church was fun. However, when I came home from college my church experience was a little different. It was not fun; but, it was good. It was uplifting and encouraging, especially since I had so many positive things going on in my life. I can honestly say as a young adult trying to navigate my way through the challenges of growing up in Baltimore City, the church saved my life. I left church every week inspired and feeling good about myself.

During that time I was not actively involved in the church. I went to service then went home. From my seat in the pew, I considered church to be perfect; everyone smiled at each other, and from the looks of it, got along. It was not until I started joining ministries and attending church meetings that I discovered another side of the church. Some of the same people who appeared so nice on Sunday mornings were "carrying on" at the church meetings. It was so bad I vowed to never attend another church meeting. It was discouraging to see people act that way while discussing church business. I was very disappointed, especially given that I had held meetings at my job with less confusion. Furthermore, a lot of the folks on my job at that time were not Christians.

My perspective towards church folks really started changing when I began serving on ministries. It was then I discovered you really do not get to know the character of the people in the church simply by attending Sunday morning service. When you start participating more and serving on ministries, you build relationships and get to know more about the church. For instance, I did not know some members had issues with new members coming in and working until I started being more active. Likewise, I did not know people fought and fussed over a lot of small things such as colors, titles and positions until I got more involved. Coming from the streets, I never experienced people fussing over church colors and who was going to be in charge. I had witnessed people fight over drug corners and money; but, colors and titles were new to me and I did not see the point. In one particular situation, I was shocked when one lady left the church and talked badly about the members all because the color she wanted to wear was not chosen. This was absolutely absurd. I had to remember what my grandmother told me as a child: just because someone goes to church does not mean they are Christ-like or perfect.

The lady who left the church because of a color is just one example of conflict. I am sure many of you know stories where people have left the church over similar minute issues and various other types of conflict. My issue is not that people leave their church because of conflict, for it happens all the time. What I do have a hard time understanding is how people allow their issues or disappointments with the church push them to give up on God. There are countless people throughout the world who have had a bad experience at church. As a result of the later, not only did they leave the church, they totally turned their backs on God. Some have even gone as far as to blame God for how they were treated and what people did to them at church.

I have always had an issue with the following: How could someone who claims to be a committed Christian give up on God because of something that happened at church? Some have done so because the pastor made a decision they did not like. Still, others because they were mistreated by someone in leadership or the church did not agree with their sexual orientation. Additionally, people have walked away from the faith because another member said something about them that were not true, or a close friend betrayed their trust. They allowed their disappointments with people to make them forfeit their relationship with God. Let me be clear, I am not seeking to minimize anyone's pain or to be insensitive about what anyone may have experienced. Yet, what people need to realize is we should never blame or give up on God because of the actions of His people. We should never stop serving or isolating ourselves from God because His people have treated us wrong. I fully understand that people in the church can cause some overwhelming pain in your life. However, being hurt by God's people is not a reason to give up on God.

We must understand that rejecting God does not hurt the church. Neither does it hurt the person or persons who have done you wrong. It only hurts you. Disconnecting yourself from God only creates a greater void in your life. It becomes difficult or almost impossible for you to overcome your pain. If you desire to overcome a bad church experience, you will need God. If you are going to bounce back from the emotional pain caused by others in the church, you are going to need God. Getting beyond your pain and overcoming church hurt is not an easy process, nor is it one you can deal with on your own. With that said, if you have been hurt, especially in the church, I encourage you to stick with God. He will get you through!

Getting Beyond the Pain and Moving on

Let me make a bold declaration. No matter how bad someone in the church has hurt you, with the Lord's help, you can overcome and move on with your life. When I say you can overcome the pain or the church hurt you have endured, I am not speaking from a theory or what I have heard, I am speaking from my personal experience. Years ago I personally experienced the pain of church hurt. It was one of the most challenging times in my life and ministry. It was such a challenge it almost caused me to walk away from the church and quit preaching the ministry. One reason I was so hurt stemmed from the surprise of it coming from people in leadership. For some strange reason I thought because someone had a title or was in a high position he or she would always exemplify Christ-like character and treat people the right way. However, I discovered having a title or a position does not guarantee a Christ-like character or that one operates with integrity. I also discovered people in high places get jealous just like everybody else.

What I went through as a new minister almost caused me to abort the calling on my life. I am forever grateful to Rev. Dr. Anthony M. Chandler, Sr.; despite not being my pastor at the time, he helped me through that challenging time. It was with his guidance and God's help I was able to forgive those who mistreated me and move forward with my life and ministry. It took a lot of prayer, personal reflection, and some wise counsel; however, I was eventually able to move beyond it and release the bitterness in my heart.

I share this experience because I am a firm believer in the need to forgive and move beyond your pain is very important as a child of God. It is necessary to all of us as believers because it is what God commands. The Bible says in Colossians 3:13, "Bear with each other and forgive one another if any of you has a grievance against someone. Forgive as the Lord forgave you." It also says in Matthew 6:14-15, "For if you forgive other people when they sin against you, your heavenly Father will also forgive you. But if you do not forgive others their sins, your Father will not forgive your sins." The need to forgive is, first of all, an act of obedience to the Word of God.

Secondly, it is important for every believer to be able to forgive and overcome their disappointments. If you do not deal with your disappointments and heal from your pain, you will eventually become bitter and start taking your issues out on others. Lastly, if you do not deal with your inner pain, it is likely you will become just like the very people you despise. It has been proven that wounded people become the oppressors if they do not deal with their pain and emotional issues. Unfortunately, there are a lot of Christians who are hurting other people largely because they have not dealt with their own pain.

If I can push this a little further, there are some churches hurting or fighting their new pastor simply because they have never healed or dealt with the pain suffered under their previous pastor. On the other hand, there are some pastors who are oppressive and mistreat their new congregations because of the way they were treated by their previous congregations. My main point is when we fail to deal with our pain and wounds, we can become just like the people who hurt us and end up inflicting our pain on others.

When a believer experiences hurt of any kind, especially in the church, we must follow Jesus' example and respond the way He did when He was being crucified on the cross. When the government and religious establishment were crucifying Him on Calvary, Jesus did not hold it against them. The Bible says He talked with God and said, "Father forgive them because they know not what they do" (Luke 23:34). Wow! Jesus, the Messiah, the Son of the Living God, who came to take away the sins of the world is being crucified and treated in a way that no man should have ever been treated. To make matters worse, He is being crucified and abused by the people He came to save. However, Jesus did not change His mind and inflict punishment on them. The Bible tells us regardless of what they did to Him, Jesus forgave His persecutors and still died for their sins. He forgave the very people who punched, spit, cursed, falsely accused and tormented Him. When Jesus was being crucified, He provided all of us an example of how to deal with people who mistreat us.

Therefore, just like Christ forgave His persecutors, we have to forgive ours. This means we have to forgive the people who wronged, lied, betrayed and did evil things to us. I can hear you saying, "I don't know if I can do that!" While I'm not saying it will be easy, with God's help you can do it. The Bible says you can do all things through Christ who gives "you" strength (Phil. 4:13). When you have been hurt or betrayed, instead of seeking revenge or holding onto a grudge, you must do what Jesus did. Namely, forgive the person(s) so that you will be free and able to move on with your life!

Now, here is the hard part. We are commanded by God to forgive, even if the person who hurt us does not say sorry or show any remorse. If they never apologize for what they have done or act oblivious to the fact that they have caused you pain, you must still forgive. Remember, forgiveness is not based on whether or not the person is apologetic or remorseful. Forgiveness is based on your obedience to God's Word. God commanded us to forgive (Eph. 4:32) and His command was not conditional. He did not tell us to only forgive if the person who hurt us said sorry or felt badly about what they did. He did not say only forgive if the person pays restitution. He instructed us to forgive those who have done us wrong. God said it. It is our job is to obey His command and that's the end of it.

Nevertheless, I recognize this is a struggle for a lot of people; even God-fearing Christians. Forgiving someone who has hurt you is not an easy thing to do, especially if he or she has not apologized. It is even more difficult to forgive when that person continues to do evil things or repeatedly betray your trust. But even as hard as it is, we as believers are still commanded to forgive. No matter how many times a person hurts us or does something negative to us, we are still expected to extend forgiveness; particularly if we are going to walk in obedience to God's Word. Therefore, if you are ready to move forward and get beyond your painful experience of church hurt, let's go!

Chapter One

Church Hurt

Chapter One

Church Hurt

"If being hurt by the church causes you to give up on God; then, your faith was in people not in God"- unknown author

THROUGH THE YEARS, I have heard many horror stories about how people were hurt by people in the church. Admittedly, I did not give it much thought because it had never happened to me. I personally did not face any real challenges or problems in church until I accepted my call to the preaching ministry. It was then that I experienced what many people call "church hurt." Here is my story. On March 1, 2002, I preached my initial sermon and was licensed as a minister of the gospel. After accepting the call to ministry, my life changed immensely. Not only did I become a minister, I also assumed the role of spiritual leader to my family and many of my childhood and college friends. While it was indeed a tremendous honor, it also added pressure for me to be an example for others to follow.

Shortly after entering the gospel ministry, I was elevated to the position of Youth and Young Adult Minister. This was an exciting and challenging assignment. I was required to lead the very individuals with whom I had previously socialized. Gradually, the Youth and Young Adult Ministry started to experience growth in numerous ways. Attendance in Sunday school and youth Bible study increased. The youth choir expanded and a youth usher board was established. In addition, the Ministry formed an after-school mentoring program for young people in our church and the community. Subsequently, the Youth and Young Adult Ministry became the catalyst largely responsible for the church's resurgence.

As the youth ministry grew, so did the church's overall membership, as many of the young people were bringing relatives and friends to church. Given the fact that the Ministry was growing and touching the lives of many; one would think that everyone, especially the pastor and leaders, would be pleased. Yet, ironically, such was not the case. This evidence of church growth seemed to be the stimulus for tension and animosity directed at me by my pastor and other leaders at the church. The following months became extremely troubling and stressful for me as the youth and young adult minister. Although ministry had become extremely troubling and taxing for me, God had begun to open doors for me to minister at other churches. Within the first two months of being licensed, I received numerous invitations to preach at various churches throughout the city.

As time passed, the situation grew worse. Although I had only been preaching for a few months, I already felt like quitting. I heard many stories of individuals who had been hurt by their pastor or church leadership, but now I had experienced it firsthand. Hurting and lacking the support I needed at my church, I reached out to another local pastor for guidance and instruction. For the next few months, I spent time with Dr. Anthony M. Chandler Sr. who ministered to me throughout this painful process. He encouraged me to stay faithful and pray for my pastor; but never say anything bad about my pastor.

After several months of praying and seeking guidance, I believed God was leading me to transition to another ministry. When I shared how I felt with my family and friends none of them thought it was a good idea. However, I expected that type of reaction since I had never disclosed how stressful ministry had become for me at my present church. When I decided I was going to leave some of the members told me if I left, I would not make it in ministry. They said I would never be successful. Hearing words like these from people I initially admired stung worse than a slap in the face. Yet and still, I had a sense of peace with my decision because I felt that I had done nothing wrong and had faithfully served my church. During my final meeting with my pastor, I thanked her for giving me my start in ministry and wished her well as she continued to lead God's people. Even though it was one of the most painful trials I had ever experienced, it helped make my transition easier.

In August 2002, I left my church and joined the New Bethlehem Baptist Church in Baltimore, Maryland under the leadership of Dr. Anthony M. Chandler Sr. Through prayer and the support of Dr. Chandler, I was able to endure one of the most emotionally draining periods of my life and move forward. While serving at New Bethlehem, I was very skeptical about building a close relationship with my new pastor. I was hesitant because I did not want to repeat the experience I had at my previous church. Dr. Chandler did not deserve my skepticism. As a result of my past pain, I built a wall of protection around me. Over time I truly got to know Dr. Chandler and saw his integrity. At that point, I removed the wall of protection and opened myself up to receive what he had to offer. That was the beginning of a healthy spiritual father and son relationship. It was one that changed my life forever.

My story, although painful, ended up being a blessing in disguise. You see, what I went through at my first church opened the door for me to go to my second church. It was at my second church that God took me places I would have never imagined. I had a Joseph moment: what some meant for evil God turned it around for my good (Genesis 50:20). However, I realized that not all experiences of church hurt have a happy and positive ending; some have ended with negative feelings. Many people who have experienced some form of church hurt have ill feelings towards the church or have left the church altogether. Unfortunately, some people have even given up on their relationship with God. These are just some of the negative effects of what we call church hurt.

This makes me raise the question, what is "church hurt?" We hear it all the time and many people claim to have experienced it, but what exactly is church hurt? It is a challenge to define because there is not a solid definition depending on to whom you talk. If you ask five different people, you will probably receive five different definitions. For instance, a pastor who I interviewed described it as "being betrayed my members and leaders of the church." Gospel artist Erica Campbell says church hurt "occurs when you've been a victim of a total abuse of power in the church. This abuse of power could be anything from sexual assault and molestation to psychological manipulation." Another person says, "Church hurt is when you are abused by the pastor or mistreated by other churchgoers." Yet another person says, "Church hurt is when people in the church do or say things to intentionally hurt you or they do not accept you for who you are." As we can see there are multiple ways that people define church hurt. However, the one thing that is consistent is when a person feels they have been mistreated by the pastor, leaders or members of the church, they call it church hurt.

I have a challenge with the term church hurt. I am not altogether sure everything identified as church hurt is actually church hurt. For example, is being rebuked by your pastor or another leader church hurt, especially if you are wrong? When someone does not allow you to have your way or they tell you no, is that church hurt? When you get replaced in a position you believed you should occupy forever is that church hurt? If someone else is chosen for a position you wanted, is that church hurt? My answer is "No." None of us will get our way all the time. Disappointments a person en-

Joseph
Pit
prison
palace

counters in the church do not mean they are being hurt by the church. These things are simply a part of ministry. We have to be careful what we label as church hurt. Not everyone is hurt by the church. Disagreements with another person or decisions not going your way should not be labeled as church hurt.

However, church hurt can manifest itself in many ways. For instance, if members of the church mistreat you because your sexual orientation is different than what they consider to be normal; that can be a form of church hurt. Or when they push you away from the church and publicly disgrace you because you had a child out of wedlock. Let's say you have been sexually assaulted and the church members side with the assailant because he or she is a long-time member and a faithful tither; that's a form of church hurt. There was a lot of love and kindness from the church members until they found out you were convicted of a felony and spent some time in prison. What about the time you shared your personal struggles, in confidence, with the pastor or another leader of the church and they, in turn, shared it with some other members? Instead of members praying for you and helping you persevere through life's storms, you became the latest member on the gossip mill.

These are just a few examples of incidents that have caused members to have ill feelings towards the church or pushed them away altogether. A lot of the people I interviewed acknowledged they have experienced church hurt because their trust was betrayed. They have been abused, assaulted, unfairly judged or mistreated by members and persons in authority. One individual stated, "I never thought people in the church would treat me worse than people in the street. I thought the church would accept me just the way I was. I guess you have to be perfect in order to go to church." The bottom line is many people have experienced some form of disappointment and hurt while at church and many others will at some point in their life. As long as the church is full of imperfect people, it will always have some type of problem. We have all sinned. Instead of gossiping and passing judgment, pray for those in the church who are struggling with a problem. It is my prayer that the actions of a few Christians do not push you away from Christ!

Discussion Questions

1. How do you define "church hurt?"

2. Did your experience of "church hurt" make you want to leave your church or leave churches altogether? If so, why?

3. Did your experience of "church hurt" impact your relationship with God? If so, how?

4. Can "church hurt" be avoided? — No

5. What advice do you have for someone who experienced any form of "church hurt?"— Pray

43

Chapter Two

Wounded by God's People

Chapter Two

Wounded by God's People

"Your slave is in your hands," Abram said. "Do with her whatever you think best." Then Sarai mistreated Hagar; so she fled from her-
Genesis 16:6

ALL OVER THE WORLD there are countless people with sad stories of how they have been hurt by someone in the church. This leaves many victims devastated and perplexed. They never expected to suffer betrayal or any form of mistreatment at church or at the hands of God's people. One of the factors that lead to victims being devastated and perplexed is their flawed expectations. A lot of people have been hurt or let down because they did not expect a person who attends church to behave in such a way that contradicts Christ-like character. I heard someone say to another person, "I can't believe she acts like that. She is supposed to be a Christian." I am quite sure many of you have heard those statements in your lifetime, especially when a believer does something another person does not like or agree with.

The problem with statements such as this is many people are under the impression that being a Christian makes you perfect. They believe when a person gives their life to Christ they will no longer sin and all their negative proclivities immediately change. People need to understand accepting Christ as your Lord and Savior does not make you make you incapable of poor decisions or actions. It also does not mean you will do everything right. Salvation means you have been saved from the penalty of sin. It does not mean you have been fully delivered from the practice of sin. Christians fall short and do things that are not pleasing to God. God's people are not infallible. They are just ordinary people who put their faith in a perfect God. Even God's people can hurt others and make bad decisions.

Do not be shocked if a person who goes to church every Sunday displays some carnal behaviors. Do not be surprised if a preacher, deacon, deaconess, trustee, usher, choir member, musician, or missionary does something mean-spirited or says something not deemed Christ-like. Let me be clear: I am not in any way condoning any carnal behaviors, I am simply pointing out these behaviors happen everywhere-- even in the church. But it is our hope that the closer we get to Christ many of our carnal behaviors will change. With that said, we will no longer behave in ways that will push someone away from Christ or the church.

Keep in mind that people who have titles are not faultless or incapable of hurting other people. Their titles have to do with their service not their sanctification. Persons holding titles do not have it all together nor are they holier than anyone else. People with titles can be just as evil, conniving and ungodly as everybody else. A lot of churchgoers have been hurt and disappointed because they assumed the person with the title would never do anything evil to hurt them. We have to remember that a title solidifies your authority for service, it does not make you sanctified and without error. Throughout history a majority of the cases of misconduct in the church have been caused by people with titles. Therefore, we should never put people on a pedestal because they have a title. Everyone, whether they have a title or not, can make a bad decision and do something to hurt another person.

A Biblical Example

Acts of betrayal or pain caused by God's people is not something that just started taking place in the 21st century. Evil acts and pain inflicted by God's people have been going on since biblical times. For example, Cain killed his brother Abel because God accepted Abel's sacrifice over his own (Genesis 4). Joseph brothers stripped him of his coat of many colors and sold him into Egypt (Genesis 37). These are just two examples of what happens when God's children allow jealousy to control their minds and actions.

Another biblical example of a person being hurt by God's people takes place in the story of Abram, Sarai, and their maidservant, Hagar. It all started in a little town called Ur of the Chaldeans. Ur was a pagan city located on the southern tip of Mesopotamia. The Bible tells us in Genesis, Chapter 12 Abram and Sarai were enjoying their peaceful and prosperous life as husband and wife. However, all of that changed when God showed up and gave Abram some strange instructions. God ordered Abram to leave his comfort zone, which was his hometown, and go to a strange land that God would show him. God told Abram He would make him into a great nation and He would bless him greatly. He also told him He would make his name great and he would be a blessing. If that was not enough, God told Abram He will bless those who blessed him and curse those who cursed him and all the peoples on Earth will be blessed through him. The Bible says without any hesitation, Abram left just as the Lord told him.

Allow me to use my biblical imagination for a moment. I imagine Abram went home and told his wife to "Pack up, we're leaving and going to a new place." To which Sarai probably queried, "But Ab, honey, where are we going?" Abram would have responded, "No clue, cause God didn't give me any of that information. He told me He'll show me when I get there. "Amazingly, Sarai did not fuss or complain. She packed up all her belongings and went with her husband. Sarai probably said to herself, I really don't understand what my husband is doing; but since I know he's following God, I don't mind following him. Although they had no idea where God was leading them, Abram and Sarai left their place of comfort and followed God's instructions. However, they also did something they would regret later. They took Abram's nephew, Lot!

Abram, Saria, Lot and their herdsmen went on this faith journey to the place God directed them. After some time had passed, God blessed Abram and Lot so much that it eventually started causing problems between the two. The land was not big enough to contain both men and their possessions. Realizing a problem was brewing, Abram went to his nephew, Lot, telling him he did not desire for tensions to get any worst between the two men. Ultimately, he decided the best thing to do was separate and go in different directions. Abram said, Lot because I love you, what I'm going to do is let you chose which way you want to go first. If you go left, I'll go right. If you go right, I'll go left. Lot, being the kind of person he was, looked up and saw the land near Jordan looked better so he chose that land for himself. He chose the land near Jordan because it looked better on the outside. What Lot did not understand is that even though the land *looked* better, it was not better. The land he chose was connected to Sodom and Gomorrah. Lot only saw what was on the outside, but he had no idea what was going on inside of that town. A lesson we can all learn from Lot is we have to be careful about making choices based on how things look on the outside because looks can be deceiving.

I'm sure many of you can attest to that statement. All of us at one point or another have discovered what some of our older relatives told us was true, "Everything that looks good to you is not always good for you." I heard one older gentleman say, "Be careful about choosing something based on how it looks. The grass may be greener on the other side, but the water bill is higher." Forrest Gump said, "My mom always said, life was like a box of chocolates, you never know what you gonna get." The point is this; we must be careful and particular about the choices we make in life. We should never settle for something because it appeals to our eyes. It could be an attractive headache! Lot learned this lesson the hard way. The land he chose looked better, but it caused him major problems and almost cost him his life (Genesis 19).

The story goes on to say after Abram and Lot separated, God spoke to Abram a second time. He said, "Look around from where you are, to the north and south, to the east and west. All the land that you see I will give to you and your off-spring forever. I will make your offspring like the dust of the earth, so if anyone can count the dusk, then your offspring could be counted" (Genesis 13:14-16).

Yet looking ahead to Chapter 15, the Bible says, Abram had a heart to heart conversation with God. He said, God I hear what you saying about my offspring and how blessed I am going to be. There is one problem, my wife and I do not have any children. Abram said, we have been trying to have children, but my wife is barren. I'm getting old and it does not seem like we are going to have a child. That was a problem for Abram because not having a son meant his inheritance would go to an outsider. When God heard Abram's concerns He said, Abram that is not something you need to worry about because you will have a son from your own body as your heir. God said, Abram just like the stars in the sky, so shall your offspring be (Genesis 15:3-5).

What God told Abram did not make any logical sense because of all of the impossibilities. However, despite of all the obstacles they would have to overcome, Abram believed God. This was a case of extreme faith since Abram knew he was old; he also knew his wife was barren. More importantly, he also knew that for the last 45-55 years they had tried to have children, but could not. In spite of his age and his wife's difficulties, he still trusted God. He still believed God could do the impossible, and because of his belief it was credited to him as righteousness. Due to his faith in God, he became the father of the faith. Abram teaches us, as believers, if we are going to receive some supernatural blessings from God, we have to trust His Word regardless of how crazy it may seem. If God said it, we must believe it!

The Danger in Trying to Help God

In Chapter 16, Abram and Sarai once again did something they would regret later. After God made the promise to Abram, years had gone by and still nothing had happened. No morning sickness, no strange food cravings, no protruding stomach, which meant Sarai was still not pregnant. To be exact, ten years had passed with no changes. When it appeared God was not going to do what he promised, Abram and Sarai did the worst thing anybody could ever do--they decided to "help" God. Sarai came up with a human solution to their problem because in their minds God was taking too long. She went to her husband and said, honey, I know how bad you want a son and I know God promised you a son, but it appears He is not able to do what He said. Therefore, I came up with a plan of my own. Sarai went on to say, since I'm unable to bear a child I want you to "hook up" with my maidservant, Hagar, and we can build a family through her. In Sarai's mind, this would solve her issue; however, it actually created more problems.

When I first read this story, I was positive that Abram being a man of faith and a man who believed God could do the impossible would tell his wife, No, we must wait on God. I just knew in my heart Abram would say this was a bad idea. But, the Bible says Abram did exactly what his wife told him to do. He said, since you insist, I'm going to follow your instructions, and he slept with Hagar. Saria's plan worked because when he slept with Hagar, the Bible says she conceived. Can you say "bad move?!" The reason being, when you fully trust God you do not move before God, neither do you alter the plan of God. When you fully trust God, you wait on Him no matter how long it takes. Abram made a terrible decision. Instead of waiting on God, he listened to his wife's instructions and tried to help God, which led to Hagar's pregnancy.

Now, one might think Hagar's being pregnant was not such a bad thing. After all, Abram and Sarai finally had their desired a son. A son, whom they can build a family around and to whom they could give their inheritance. However, life did not go the way they planned, for they actually created more problems within the family. After Hagar became pregnant, her attitude towards Sarai changed. Hagar began to despise Sarai and started acting different towards her. Perhaps, Hagar started acting funny because she could provide Abram something Saria could not. If that was not the case, maybe she started thinking: Since I'm pregnant, I can take Sarai's place and become the first lady of the First Baptist Church of Ur. However, the plan backfired on everyone involved. Due to Hagar's attitude toward Sarai, the Bible says Sarai got angry at Abram. Yes, you read it right. Hagar started acting foolish toward Sarai and Sarai got angry at Abram. Yes, this may sound like one of those television reality shows, but this is a real story in the Bible.

When Hagar started outwardly disrespecting Sarai, Sarai got an attitude with Abram and told him he was responsible for the wrong she was suffering. She said "I put my servant in your arms, and now that she knows she is pregnant, she despises me" (Genesis 16:5). Poor Abram; all he did was what his wife Sarai begged him to do and now the poor man was in trouble. Abram was confused because his wife was angry with him and blaming him for her unhappiness. All he had done was listened to his wife. He could not understand why Sarai was mad at him when Hagar was the one acting out. His wife came up with the plan, Abram followed it, Hagar started acting out and somehow Abram gets all the blame. Certainly, when you lose patience and try to help God things get messy and people end up getting hurt. The lesson we should take from this situation is to wait on God and never alter God's plan to fulfill your own purpose in life!

Wounded by God's People

Here is where the story gets worse. Instead of Abram resolving the conflict, he tried to avoid it by getting rid of it. Let's examine what he said in Genesis 16:6, he told his wife "Hagar was in her hands and she could do with her whatever she thought was best." Using my biblical imagination, I believe what he was really saying to Sarai was, Do with her whatever you desire, just don't put me in the middle of it. That's exactly what Sarai did. The Bible says, "Sarai mistreated Hagar." She dealt with her harshly. It was so bad that Hagar packed up and fled from Abram's house. Hagar was wounded and hurt by God's people.

Have you ever been mistreated by God's people? Have you ever been made to feel like you were nothing at all? Hagar must have felt used, abused and betrayed when she fled from Abram and Sarai. It was really painful because she thought the father of her soon to be child would defend her, but he stood by and did nothing. Hagar was devastated and hurt at the hands of "God's people." She did what many people do when they get hurt in church, she left and vowed to never serve them again. I imagine as she was on her way home to a small town in Egypt, she wished she never tried to help them. I'm sure Hagar was shattered when they started mistreating her. Hagar said, I made one bad decision and now they are treating me like I'm the worst person in the world. They act like they never messed up or made a bad decision. The hurt and devastation she felt ultimately caused her to run away from the place she used to call home. Hagar was so hurt, that she not only ran away from God's people; she was giving up on their God.

When I read this story it made me wonder how many people have run away from the church after being mistreated by God's people? How many people have left the church and vowed to never return, because after one bad decision they were criticized and ostracized by God's people? How many people have ever felt like giving up on God because of the way they were treated by His people? Unfortunately, there are countless people who just like Hagar, have been hurt or mistreated by some of God's people. They have not only left the church, but the faith altogether.

It's sad to say this, but some "church folks" can be cruel. Some church folks can be mean and nasty to other people. Church folks can be something else. If you think I'm not being truthful, just start hanging around and start getting involved in ministry. You will see exactly what I'm talking about. You can be put on a pedestal one minute, but as soon as you make one mistake, they will want to try to bury you. They will celebrate you when you are doing well, but crucify you the minute you mess up. Some church folk will treat you so bad that it will make you want to leave church and never come back.

I do not know if you have ever felt like this, but I have had my share of days where I wanted to resign and never step foot in a church again. Keep me in your prayers because if

I'm entirely honest, I have had a few days where I wanted to lay hands on some people—and I do not mean praying. If you find yourself unable to relate and have never been mistreated or hurt by church folks, just keep on living, your day will come. Some church folks can be cruel and mean-spirited towards you, especially if you mess up!

Here is what's perplexing about some people in the church: they will judge you and make you out to be the worst person in the world because you messed up, as if they have never messed up. They will spread gossip about you and your bad decisions as if they have never done the same. They will shame you for your sins as if they are without sin. Each person in the church regardless of how long he or she has been saved, the title or position held, has messed up at one time or another. All of us have fallen short of the glory of God and made some bad decisions. All of us have done something we wish we would never have done. Therefore, if no one else has compassion on people who have fallen, we as believers should have compassion. We are all recipients of grace. This is a good place to stop reading and say, Amen!

Similarly, Hagar made one bad decision and Sarai and Abram threw her by the wayside. Instead of dismissing her, they should have corrected her with love and moved on. After all, she was trying to help them. Yet, instead of handling it in a godly and forgiving way, the Bible says they mistreated her; which resulted in her fleeing back to Egypt. It was at this point that Hagar discovered something about God. She learned that despite her flaws and mistakes the Lord still cared about her. As she was walking back to Egypt, she stopped and took a water break at a well located in the desert of Shur. While she was weeping at the well, the angel of the Lord found Her near a spring in the desert and told her to go back to her mistress for God would take care of her. God wanted Hagar to know that although she had been mistreated she still had value.

Likewise, I want every person who has been mistreated or wounded by God's people to know you are still valuable and loved by God. People may have abused, hurt or ridiculed you. They may have overlooked you or even tried to devalue your worth, but God still loves you and cares about you. Do not let the actions of God's people push you away from God or His house. Remember, no matter how bad God's people may have treated you or what they have done to hurt you, it does not diminish who you are. You are still valuable to God!

Discussion Questions

1. What are some of the things we do that hurt others in the church?

2. What could Sarai and Abram have done differently in regard to how they handled Hagar?

3. As a church, what can we do to make sure people do not give up on God when they are hurt by God's people?

Chapter Three

I'm Leaving Because I Don't Like the Pastor

Chapter Three

I'm Leaving Because I Don't Like the Pastor

RECENTLY, I read an article by Chuck Lawless entitled, "12 REASONS WHY PEOPLE LEAVE A LOCAL CHURCH." It was an interesting read in that it helped shed light on a few questions I have been wrestling with over the last year. In this article, Lawless gives these 12 reasons why people leave the church:

1. **Relationship conflict**. Somebody got mad at somebody else, and one (or both) of them decided to find another church.

2. **Weak preaching**. A congregation will put up with a lot of poor leadership, but many—especially young people—will not sit long under poor preaching.

3. **Authoritarian leadership.** Some leaders do not permit opposing views, and they expect everyone to follow in line. In turn, some members simply don't stay under that leadership style.

4. **Poor children's or students' programming**. Even though it's not good, it's one thing for adults to have little opportunities for growth; it's another matter completely when our church provides little for our children and young people.

5. **Neglected pastoral care.** Right or wrong, some church members give their pastors only one shot at pastoral care. If the pastor somehow neglects a need, members start looking elsewhere.

6. **Personal sin.** Sometimes it's easier to leave a church than to sit under preaching that convicts week after week after week...which also means it's apparently easier to leave than it is to repent.

7. **Burnout.** Members who are really faithful to a local church at times overcommit themselves based on the needs of the church. Few people are willing to admit they're just worn out, so some will simply leave instead.

8. **No connectedness.** Lonely church members— regardless of whether they're lonely because the church is unfriendly or because they choose not to get involved—don't usually commit for the long haul in a church.

9. **Congregational strife.** Even if you're not in the middle of the battle, constant conflict wears out even the best church members.

10. **Theological disagreement.** Sometimes this difference is over actual theological beliefs, and sometimes it's over moral right and wrong.

11. **Political positions.** Granted, this reason is often more apparent during campaign seasons, but it happens.

12. **Perceived irrelevance**. Members who think the preaching and teaching do not speak to the reality of their day-to-day lives will often seek that kind of teaching elsewhere.

Reading these 12 reasons caused me to continue the conversation and look more into this matter. I reached out to a few individuals who had recently left their church to get their feedback on this topic. Many of the people I spoke with agreed with these twelve reasons, but it was another reason that continued to come up. Many of them stated they left their church because they did not like their pastor. These individuals left their church, went to another church or stopped going to church altogether due to how they felt about the pastor.

What I found quite shocking was some of the people who said they left because they did not like the pastor could not articulate anything negative the pastor did to them. Some stated they did not like the pastor because of the changes made in the church. Others did not like the preaching. Some were mad because the pastor moved them out of "their" position or did not visit them when they were in the hospital. I was really blown away when I heard one person say, "I left because I did not like his wife and he always talked about her."

When I heard these sentiments, I tried not to minimize or negate what they were feeling. My question to them was, "Are those reasons to leave your church?" When things do not go your way or the pastor makes a decision you do not agree with, is that a reason to leave the church you love and grew up attending? If the pastor sends a deacon to visit you in the hospital or gets a missionary to call to check on you instead of personally coming, is that a reason not to like your pastor or leave your church? Furthermore, if the pastor chooses to replace you after 15 to 20 years of service in the same position, is that a reason to not like your pastor or leave your church? There are many people who dislike their pastor for various reasons. The question still remains, is that a reason to leave your church? Can you and your pastor work through the problems? Or have you even tried to work it out?

In many circumstances, people get angry at the pastor and leave the church without any attempts to resolve the issue. Many pastors have been blamed for not caring about members' concerns. Yet, some members have never discussed their concerns with the pastor. No one can address an issue they have no knowledge of. Pastors have been blessed with many gifts and talents, but one gift or talent I do not believe any pastor has is the ability to "read minds." Therefore, if you have a problem with your pastor, before leaving the church, perhaps you should discuss it with them, and prayerfully it can be worked out.

Additionally, I discovered not every member who has an issue with the pastor leaves the church; some stay and intentionally show their displeasure. Often times, these are the ones who do not like or agree with anything going on in the church. They do not support anything the church does. They do not give tithes and offerings, for they are of the mindset the money goes to the pastor. They come to church every Sunday and sit in the sanctuary with a bitter deposition while the pastor preaches. They never say amen during the pastor's sermon. On the flip side, they are overly excited and extremely loud when there is a guest preacher. Everyone in the congregation knows they dislike the pastor because they have readily made it known.

What these individuals fail to understand is sitting in the congregation with an attitude and demonstrating their displeasure is not hurting the pastor or messing up the pastor's day; in truth, it actually ruins their own worship experience. I cannot speak for any other pastor, but it does not bother me or disrupt my sermon when people sit in service frowning or acting disinterested when I preach. I just continue to deliver the Word of God.

When I was younger, I used to let things like that bother me and I would go home stressed and try to figure out why a person would act that way, especially in worship. I had many nights when I could not sleep because I was upset about what someone said about me. I pondered why people acted as though they did not like me. God has delivered me from worrying about whether people like me or not. He also delivered me from trying to please everybody and make everyone think well of me. As a pastor, I try my best to lead my congregation with integrity, show everyone respect, and engage all of my members. I realize in this profession not everyone is going to be happy with me or even nice to me. This is fine. As long as we can be respectful to each other, I can deal with their feelings and still treat them with respect.

Be Committed to the Church, Not the Pastor

One of the mistakes I think many believers make is they choose a church solely on the pastor, not the culture of the church. If they like the way pastor preaches, they immediately join the church without considering the culture or mission of the church. They do not inquire about the ministries of the church to ensure it meets their spiritual and emotional needs. If they like the pastor, it becomes the church God has for them. Now, let me be clear: the pastor and the ability to minister to you through the Word of God are important. However, I do not think it should be the only factor one considers when choosing a church home. If you choose a church solely because of the pastor, you will be committed to the pastor and not the church.

When people chose churches merely because of the pastor, they create an idol rather than a Shepherd. That is not a good thing. God warns us from making and worshipping idols. The Bible says in Exodus 20:3-5, "You shall have no other gods before me. You shall not make for yourself an image in the form of anything in heaven above or on the earth beneath or in the waters below. You shall not bow down to them or worship them; for I, the Lord your God, am a jealous God, punishing the children for the sin of the parents to the third and fourth generation of those who hate me."

Whether you believe it or not, some people make the pastor an idol. Some feel they cannot get a Word from God unless it comes from the pastor; as if God cannot use someone else to deliver His word. For instance, if the pastor is not there a particular Sunday, some members get upset or go back home. They do not want to hear anybody else preach but the pastor. They are the ones who say, "I would have stayed home if I knew pastor wasn't going to be here." For that very reason, many pastors do not publicly announce when they are not preaching or going to be away from their pulpit.

Additionally, it's not good to make your church membership solely about the pastor because if you and the pastor have a disagreement you will leave the church. Your connection was to him not the church. In many churches, the lead pastor comes and goes. If the pastor leaves, does that mean you have to find another church? If the pastor falls short and does something that causes him to get dismissed from the church, do you also leave the church because your connection was to the pastor, not the church?

There is nothing wrong with being a part of a church that has a "good" pastor. Nonetheless, the reason you become a member should not be solely based on the pastor. Certainly, the pastor should be one of the reasons you join a church, but it should not be the only reason. This can lead to an unhealthy church experience.

Help! I Dislike My Pastor!

No matter what church you attend, there will always be a few people who do not like the pastor. It's inescapable reality. The problem is not how they feel about the pastor; people are entitled to feel how they desire. But rather, the problem lies in how they act and treat the pastor because of those feelings. Some church members mistreat, lie, ridicule, and even disrespect the pastor because of their dislike. I am a firm believer that regardless of how you feel about the pastor, you should still respect and honor the position.

In addition, I believe it is a dangerous thing to speak against and do negative things to one of God's chosen vessels. For example, in Numbers, Chapter 12, God punished Miriam and Aaron because they spoke against His servant Moses. The Bible also says in Psalm 105:15, "Do not touch my anointed ones; do my prophets no harm." You are entitled to your feelings about your pastor, but please be careful what you do and say about your pastor. Whether you like them or not, pastors are still God's chosen vessels.

Let me help those individuals who dislike or have an issue with their pastor. These are a few steps I believe you should consider rather than sitting in church with an attitude and "fighting" against your pastor.

1. **Meet with your pastor to discuss your feelings.**
   One of the worst things you can do is harbor bitterness in your heart. Meet with your pastor so that you can discuss your issues or concerns. The Bible says in Matthew 18:15, "If your brother or sister sins, go and point out their fault, just between the two of you. If they listen to you, you have won them over." Having a discussion can help resolve issues amongst two individuals and it may also reveal some things that will be helpful for moving forward. For example, I had a member who was upset with me for months because she was sick and she thought I never called to check on her. However, when we met to discuss her issue, she discovered that I called many times and left numerous messages on her house phone, but she never checked because she uses her cell. Something as small as a conversation can help mend a broken relationship.

2. **Stay positive!** If you dislike your pastor, don't attempt to make others feel the way you do. Look for ways to reconcile. Avoid gossiping and spreading negative things about the pastor to other members and the community; that only makes things worst. Always look for a solution and a way to move forward so that you can enjoy your church experience.

3. **Pray for your pastor.** Pastors need prayer. Not every decision a pastor makes is intentionally trying to hurt you. If you do not like your pastor's attitude or the way they treat members, pray for them. Prayer works. I have found that if you constantly pray for someone, it becomes harder to hold a grudge or dislike them.

4. **Extend Grace and Mercy**. Remember the grace and mercy that God has shown you, go and do likewise. All of us make mistakes and do things someone may not like. However, before you judge a person for his or her decision, spend some time to get to know them and learn why he or she made a particular decision. Doing so may give you a better understanding. Keep in mind that none of us are perfect; we all need a little grace and mercy.

5. **Be willing to work on your issues as well**. If you're asking the pastor to change, be willing to change yourself. Healthy confrontation can be a learning experience for you and the pastor. Remember to be humble as you speak with your pastor. Be open to changes that you might need to consider. A pastor will be more willing to adjust their way of thinking if they perceive a teachable spirit in you.

What to Do When You Disagree with Your Pastor

In the article entitled, "What to Do When You Disagree with Your Pastor," Paul Alexander gives four things you should do when you disagree with your pastor so that the concerns don't get messy and cause problems at your church.

1. **Choose to Love Them**

   You don't have to agree with someone in order to love them. I choose to love people I don't agree with all the time. If I didn't, I wouldn't be married. This may seem like a simple step but it's an important step.

2. Take Personal Ownership

The best place to start when you don't agree with your pastor is not with the question, "What do they need to change?" but rather, "What do I need to change?" Do I need to change my belief, assumptions, attitude, approach or actions? This is an important step, because while you can't change another person, you can change you.

3. Submit to Them

God has given a unique seat to the leader you're following, and it's important to remember that He's chosen to give that seat to them...not you. Make sure you measure your attitude and keep your heart in check. It's important to tell yourself the truth. Speaking poorly of your leader or creating disunity not only hurts the church and the movement of the Gospel, but the Bible talks about those things as sin. It wouldn't be a bad idea to remember and read up on the way David submitted to Saul. Oh yeah...and remember, even if you don't like it, for some reason God has allowed the leadership at your church to be in authority at this time. God could be using this time in your life to teach you lessons like: "learning how to be under authority before you're in authority," or "the art of timing."

4. Leave Them

If you've lost respect for your pastor and you can no longer in good conscience follow them, it may be time to leave. If you cannot submit to the leadership of your pastor or by you staying it will create disunity, it may be time to leave.

Discussion Questions

1. What do you feel is the best way to handle a disagreement with your pastor?

2. Why do some people talk about their pastor's decisions, but never talk to the pastor about them?

3. How do you move forward after a disagreement with your pastor?

4. What if you discovered that the pastor made the right decision and you were wrong? What will you do?

5. Have you considered that when you fight against the vision, you may not be fighting against the pastor, but God?

Pastor / Vision

Chapter Four

Pastors Get Hurt Too

Chapter Four

Pastors Get Hurt Too

"At my first defense, no one came to my support, but everyone deserted me.
May it not be held against them."- 2 Timothy 4:16

"Therefore, my dear brothers and sisters, stand firm. Let nothing move you. Always give yourselves fully to the work of the Lord, because you know that your labor in the Lord is not in vain."
1 Corinthians 15:58

Whenever someone talks about "church hurt" or a person being betrayed by the church, most people automatically think it's a situation concerning a member, ministry leader or a staff person. However, not all cases of church hurt and incidents of betrayal are limited to members, ministry leaders and staff; pastors get hurt too. This may be breaking news to some, but many pastors have also been victims of what we call church hurt. There are numerous pastors who have been hurt, betrayed, disappointed, lied on, mistreated, and even deceived by the church, or should I say, by people in the church. Although you do not hear a lot about pastors experiencing church hurt, it happens to them just like everybody else. In some instances, pastors face more scrutiny and unfair treatment than their members.

One of the reasons many people do not realize pastors get hurt is because they do not fully understand the pastor's world. They see the anniversaries and accolades that come with leading God's people, but they do not see the weight and responsibilities that come with such a role. They see the people loving and celebrating their pastors during service, but they have not read their emails or checked their phone messages during the week. Many people are fooled by the accolades that come with being the pastor, but they have no idea of the attacks which also come. To be clear, pastoring a church is more than having your name on the church van or marquee out front. It's more than teaching Bible study, putting on a robe, and preaching Sunday morning service. Leading God's people is one of the most stressful occupations in the world.

Pastoring is a stressful and challenging occupation for many reasons. Pastors are on call 24/7. A pastor's absence from his home or office is not an indication work is not being done or church business is not being handled. Even when pastors turn their cell phone off, their mind is still pondering the next move or mentally dealing with the challenges within the church. The pastor's job is never done! In addition, pastors are sometimes called to be part-time referees in an effort to settle disagreements. Truly, most of the fights or disagreements have nothing to do with God or the spiritual growth of the church. The majority of church fights are over power, positions, titles and committees. Stress or unrest for the pastor is created when the individuals involved do not try to resolve the issue themselves or go to a deacon for help; they go straight to the pastor.

But wait, there is more. Almost every decision the pastor makes is scrutinized and met with some resistance, especially if the decision affects a person directly or the ministry of which they are a member. Some people do not want the pastor to make any changes because they have always done "it" a certain way. They do not see why they have to do something differently, even if what they are currently doing is not working.

For most pastors, ministry is an emotional rollercoaster. This is due to the highs and lows that come with leading God's people. In addition, the ways in which members treat their pastors contribute to this emotional rollercoaster. For example, members love you and treat you like you are the best pastor in the world until you make a decision they do not like, then they treat you like you are the worst pastor in the world. When you first arrived at the church, they were happy you were there; but when they get mad at you, they want you to leave and their name is the first one to sign the petition. It's similar to Holy Week. On Sunday the people shouted "Hosanna to the Son of David! Blessed is he who comes in the name of the Lord!" (Matthew 21:9). Whereas on Friday, some of those same people shouted "Crucify him!" (Matthew 27:23).

I have learned some people's feelings about their pastor change weekly. One week they love them, the next week they cannot stand them. As a pastor, I have learned not to take it personally when members have bad feelings for me or they express their dislike of me. As long as they are members of the church, we have to love and minister to them regardless of how they feel about us. Our faithfulness to the assignment is not based on how people feel about us; it's based on our obedience to God. While it's not always easy to do, with the guidance of the Holy Spirit and a whole lot of prayer it can be done.

If They Only Knew

A few years ago, I overheard a lady in church say, "Why does the pastor need a vacation, he only works on Wednesdays and Sundays; his job is not that hard?" Unfortunately, a lot of people think the same way. They think, as pastors, we preach Sunday mornings, teach Bible study on Wednesdays and sit back and relax the rest of the week. I wish it was that easy, but that is far from the truth. I have found the preaching and teaching to be the easiest part of the job; dealing with the "other stuff" has been the challenge.

What some people do not realize is that we are held responsible for almost everything that goes on in the church. Yet many pastors have to fight other leaders to have involvement or input concerning the affairs of the church. Furthermore, many pastors get the blame when the church is not moving forward or going in the right direction. Members, however, do not consider that in some instances the pastor's hands are tied to the traditions and personal preferences of the people. It is hard to move a church forward when there is competition for power. Although the pastors are in the driver's seat, in a number of cases, they are not allowed to drive. Numerous pastors have stated it's hard for them to lead their congregation anywhere because they have members, leaders, deacons and trustees who do not want them to be involved in the major decisions of the church. This style of church government is a recipe for disaster. When God gives vision or direction for the church, it comes through the pastor. Subsequently, if the church is making moves and implementing vision without the pastor's input, it's their vision, not God's.

Moreover, I wonder if some members realize their pastor is not Superman or Wonder Woman. Every pastor has a limited time capacity. They only have 168 hours per week to do everything that needs to be done, which includes family time, proper sleep, sermon prep, Bible study, meetings, administrative duties, member visitations and regular church events. Hopefully, nothing unexpected pops up like deaths or critical accidents. If everything goes according to plan and nothing additional creeps up, the pastor may have a few minutes throughout the week to sit down and relax. Regrettably, that does not happen too often.

In most cases the issue is not the pastors' understanding that their time is limited, the issue is some members do not understand the pastor's time capacity is limited. Due to not being mindful of this, they get upset if the pastor is not available whenever they need something or want to discuss what's going on in their lives. Some members get an attitude if the pastor is busy and sends a deacon or a representative from the church to visit them in the hospital. Despite the pastor is just one person with countless responsibilities, some members expect the pastor to be at every function. Regardless of how much the pastor already has going on, some members want the pastor to be at every service, every meeting, every program, every breakfast, every luncheon, every play, every trip, and every activity that occurs at the church. Some members even expect the pastor to make all the private and family affairs as well.

As a pastor, I try to be supportive to all my members and attend as many events as I can. Still, I have my family and I have to do things for them and myself, like rest. There are times I am available to make events and attend some of the member's family affairs, but I cannot make them all. I have learned if two members are having a function at the same time and I go to one and not the other, the member whose event I did not attend will be upset and say I'm showing favoritism. Situations like this used to bother me. I did not want any member feeling I like I chose another family over theirs. There were many times I found myself running all over the place trying to attend all the functions so everybody would be happy. However, while I was making the members happy, I was neglecting my own family; hence, causing problems at home. Pastors will always have problems when their secondary ministry (the church) causes them to neglect their primary ministry (their biological family).

The first few years at Holy Trinity I have to admit, I was running myself "to death" trying to be at everything. Whenever I received an invitation from one of my members, regardless of what I had going on, I made it my business to be there to show my support. It got so bad that I was out late on Saturday nights trying to be a "good pastor." I was showing up at every event, even if it had nothing to do with church. It was not until my adopted daddy, Deacon Gatling, sat me down and told me, "You're only one person. You cannot make everything." He said, "We do not need you to be wearing yourself out trying to be at everybody's function; we need you to be ready to preach the Word on Sunday." Then he said, "You need to learn how to say 'no', and tell people you can't make it. If they don't like it, that's their issue not yours."

After having that talk with Deacon Gatling, I began to make better use of my time. I no longer feel guilty or allow someone to make me feel guilty if I cannot make their event. It took some time, but I finally realized that my time capacity was limited. I was only hurting myself and my family trying to attend everything. I also learned "No" is not a bad word; it will actually do you some good!

It's Always the Pastor's Fault

Serving as the pastor of the church comes with many accolades and high praise from members and people in the community. Whether you desire it or not, it's a part of the calling. When the church is doing well and it is growing spiritually, numerically and financially, the pastor usually gets praised for doing an amazing job. Some members even boast to family and friends they have the best pastor; a pastor with vision, who can rightly divide the Word of God. It's a given that members celebrate their pastor when the church is excelling and in a good place.

On the other hand, if the church experiences an unforeseen financial setback or a decline in membership, the majority of those praises will turn into complaints. When things are not going as well as they used to, people are quick to put blame on the pastor and say it's the pastor's fault. If a program or ministry event is not successful, for some people, it's the pastor's fault. If money stops coming in like it used to and the church goes over budget, it's the pastor's fault. If members stop coming to church, regardless of the reason behind their inconsistency, the pastor still gets blamed. Almost everything bad that happens in the church is perceived to be the pastor's fault. That is one of the challenges of being the leader, someway or somehow, it's always the pastor's fault.

That being the case, many pastors are under constant pressure to make sure that the church is growing and ministry is doing well. This becomes a major challenge in this new age church culture where people's commitment to the church is not like it used to be. The pastor plays a very important role in the growth and spiritual development of every church. But one thing we should take into consideration, it's not always the pastor's fault that a church is not growing spiritually and financially. Neither is it always the pastor's fault that people leave the church or stop giving to the church. It is true that some people leave because they have an issue with the pastor, but they also leave because of mean and nasty members. When tithes drop and people do not give consistently, it's not always because they do not like the sermons, or they are angry about a change the pastor made. Sometimes people do not give because of personal reasons. For example: they are in debt, unemployed, financially struggling or they are angry with the trustees.

The main point is, when churches experience problems and start declining it's not always the pastor's fault. There are numerous other reasons a person leaves the church or stops giving. Therefore, before the blame is put on the pastor, take time to investigate what really made the person leave or stop giving to the church. It is important because numerous pastors have been blamed for issues that people have with the church, or for members leaving the church altogether. They discover later that it had nothing to do with the pastor. I'm not suggesting that the pastor is never at fault and members never leave because of the pastor. That would not be a true statement. People do leave their churches because of issues they have with the pastor, but it's not always the pastor's fault.

I Don't Know Who I Can Trust

Recently I spoke with a senior pastor and asked him, "If you could start over what would you do differently?" He said, "If I could turn back the hands of time and start all over, the one thing I would do differently is not get as close to my members as I did at my first church." When he made that statement, it sort of shocked me. I was expecting him to talk about the mistakes he made as a young pastor or how he could have been more patient when implementing change. But to my surprise, he talked about how he would change the way he related to his members. I was intrigued by his answer so I asked him why that was important for him to change. He told me he would change it because most of the pain and hurt he suffered in ministry came from the individuals who were close to him.

As I sat there listening to him share his story, I saw the pain and hurt in his face. He mentioned he should have listened to his pastor who advised him not to become too friendly with the members of his church. His pastor told him that it was ok for him to be friendly, but he should not be their friend. Everyone may not be spiritually mature enough to handle that type of relationship with their pastor. Although it was sound advice, he ignored what his pastor told him and developed close friendships with a few of his members. He was so close to some of them they were like family.

When I asked how they became so close, he stated they were there for him when he first arrived at the church. They were extremely kind to his family and they helped him get acclimated to his new environment. He talked about how the first few years at the church they were very supportive of his ministry, and they defended him when the "naysayers and haters" tried to attack his vision and character. They were always over each other's houses, and over the summer they started traveling together. He said they were like his best friends and he was very comfortable around them. His level of comfort was due to the fact that they saw the "real him" and did not judge him when he was not functioning in his pastoral capacity. Eventually, he became so comfortable with them he began sharing personal struggles and the challenges he was having at home; thinking it would stay confidential.

However, in retrospect, he now regrets being so transparent and allowing his members to get as close to him as they did. He said things were great for a while, but he noticed a change in the relationships once he made a few of them leaders in the church. He felt that they started treating him differently and were not as supportive as they used to be after he challenged them to do better as leaders; and he would not allow them to do whatever they wanted to do at church. Things really changed when he had to discipline one of his closest "members/friends" and give him a season of rest. It hurt him to do it, but as the pastor it was a decision he had to make because his friend's behavior was completely out of control and unbecoming of a leader.

Although the individual knew he was wrong for what he did, he was still upset with the pastor, or should I say his friend, for giving him a season of rest. He felt the pastor should have ignored it and just let it go, especially since they were friends. When the pastor did what a pastor should do, regardless of the relationship, his friend was highly upset and started turning on the pastor. He started spreading the pastor's personal business around the congregation. He also became one of his biggest critics and adversaries in church meetings.

This situation eventually caused major problems for the pastor and his family. It became so bad for the pastor he resigned and went to another church. After hearing the whole story, I asked him, "What hurt you the most about the entire situation?" He said, "I felt betrayed." It was not how the congregation treated him after learning about his flaws and personal struggles, it was that one of his friends/members told them about his struggles. He said instead of helping him get through his struggles, his member used them to hurt him.

It was this situation that changed the way he interacted with his members. He said that experience caused him to become anti-social and not trust anyone in the congregation. This was one case of a pastor dealing with church hurt or betrayal, but there are numerous situations similar to his. One thing is for sure, a lot of pastors have trust issues when it comes to members. Pastors would love to just be a regular person around their members. However, many pastors do not know who they can trust enough to be transparent and share their weaknesses without hearing it again. As I noted earlier everyone cannot handle their pastor being transparent or a regular person. Therefore, it may not be that your pastor is "acting funny" or being anti-social; it could be they just do not know who they can trust.

Every Pastor Needs A Few "Real Friends"

It may seem hard to believe, but many pastors are lonely. This statement can be somewhat confusing. Congregations hear pastors say from the pulpit when introducing the guest preacher, "my friend and brother." However, for most of us, it's something we say for purpose of introduction. In reality, most of the preachers we call our friend and brother or sister are just our associates and colleagues in ministry; not genuine friends. Most pastors do not have a lot of close and genuine friends. If pastors have five good friends whom they can trust and share personal and private information, they are blessed and highly favored! Genuine friends are hard to find, but it's even harder in ministry. That being the case, many pastors confide and get close to members of their congregation.

When a pastor builds a relationship with a member of their church and allows them into their personal lives, it should be handled gracefully and prayerfully. Never forget that your pastor is human and they make mistakes just like everybody else. Therefore, do not expect them to be a perfect person. If you are a close friend with your pastor, it's because they trust you; they believe you can handle their humanity. However, if you are going to be a "real friend" to your pastor, you have to make sure your motives are pure and you are not in it for personal reasons. You cannot be a good friend to your pastor if you are doing it for personal gain or accolades. Your pastor needs people to help carry the weight of ministry and the burdens of life. Sometimes your pastor will need you to be a sounding board; a person who will just listen while they vent. Other times they will need you to be an encourager. Pastors get discouraged, frustrated and overwhelmed. Sometimes whether they admit it or not, they need a word of encouragement. As a friend, you can be that source of encouragement.

Whatever role you play as the pastor's friend, here is something you should keep in mind: he or she is still your pastor. In essence, do not allow the friendship to get in the way of the pastoral relationship. He or she was your pastor first and will remain as such as long as you are a member of the church. If you feel that being friends will hinder your ability to respect them as your pastor, perhaps, it is best if you do not become close friends. I say that because even as your friend, his or her first obligation is to be your pastor. As your pastor, he or she will have to do what's right for the church and make some decisions with which you may not like or agree. If you are a true friend, you will understand the pastor's decision and it will not hinder your loyalty. Real friends can handle rebuke from their pastor and still remain loyal.

Discussion Questions:

1. Did you realize that pastors get hurt too? -- Yes

2. Are you familiar with all that a pastor has to go through while leading a church? -- Not all

3. Should the pastor be blamed for everything that happens in the church? -- No -- Team work

4. Do you feel the pastor should get close to members of the congregation? Yes

5. What is a safe relationship for a pastor to have with their members? -- Pastor/people

87

Chapter Five

Pastors' Wives Get Hurt Too

Chapter Five

Pastors' Wives Get Hurt Too

What are these wounds? I was wounded in the house of my friends
(Zechariah 13:6).

EVERY YEAR at the beginning of June I attend the Hampton's University Ministers Conference in Hampton, Virginia. One of the things I love about attending this conference is the fellowship with other pastors from all across the country. After worship we usually go out to eat and just talk about life and ministry. There was one particular time we were eating and talking about the challenges we face as pastors and leading God's people. We debated about who had the hardest job in the world, the President of the United States or being a pastor. The waitress who was taking our orders overheard our conversation and she made a statement that shocked all of us. She said, "Leading the country and the church are both extremely hard jobs, but the person who has the hardest job in the world are pastors' wives."

Wow! When she made that statement everyone at the table was somewhat shocked because we never even considered what our wives go through in ministry. We spent the rest of our time at lunch discussing the challenges our spouses face as a pastor's wife.

As important as the pastors' wives are to pastors and their ministry, you do not hear much about the challenges they face in ministry. Sitting at that table we began to realize that the burden of being a pastor's wife is heavy. It requires strong and secure women of God to walk in those shoes. Throughout time there have been numerous horror stories concerning pastors' wives being hurt or mistreated by the church or should I say by individuals in the church. Some spouses experience so much disrespect and mistreatment they no longer attend the church their husbands pastor. One "first lady" said, I hate my church and the only reason I go is to support my husband. When someone asked why she felt that way, she stated, "Because the church is hurting my family and the people treat me unfairly."

Throughout the ages, marriages have struggled, families have been fractured and wives and their children have developed ill-feelings towards the church. The reason many families have developed bad feeling towards the church is because they feel their families are being divided by the church. No family likes being neglected or put off because of the church. The church should strengthen the families, not divide them. Many pastors' wives feel neglected and lonely because their husbands always have to be at the church. Now this is not always the churches' fault. Some pastors take on too much and do not know how to say no to anyone, except their families. However, some churches expect their pastor to be at everything and will get upset if they miss an event to spend time with family. Situations like this have caused many pastors to have problems at home and their families ended up resenting the church.

Moreover, the job as a pastor's wife can be very stressful and overwhelming at times. This is important to note because there are many pastors' wives who are suffering in silence. Although they are miserable, they force themselves to come to church and smile. They do this because they do not want to create additional problems for their husbands. Their emotional struggles cause many of them to be depressed, lonely, have physical challenges and become mentally overwhelmed. We have to keep all pastors' wives lifted up in prayer because they have one of the hardest jobs in the world. What makes it even worst is that they do not get paid for the stress and frustration they have to deal with on a regular basis. Most churches expect their pastor's wife to be very involved in the ministry. Yet, some churches never compensate or even appreciate their leading ladies for their service.

There is an article I read a while ago that I would like to share concerning the pain and burdens that come with being a pastor's wife. I felt led to share this article because it opened my eyes to some things I have never considered. The article is entitled, *Confessions of a pastor's wife: When I don't like church* by Ellen Stumbo. Here is what it says:

> I usually enjoy going to church, it is a place of renewal, encouragement, and support. Nonetheless, there have been times in life when I would like to pull away and do my own

thing, but I can't because I am a pastors' wives. So I have dragged my children to church after having a rotten morning, put on my happy face and answered, "Good!" with a big smile when people ask, "How are you this morning?" Because I know people don't really care, it has been years since someone stopped me at church and asked, "How are you really doing?" As a matter of fact, this has only happened once in my ten years in ministry. It happened three years ago, we had been home for only a couple of months after adopting Nina. I left church early, and had the girls buckled in the car when my dear friends approached me in the parking lot. "Ellen, we are worried about you. How are you really doing?" I couldn't even answer them. I broke down and began sobbing; I literally fell into their arms and cried and cried. I was not doing well at all emotionally. They helped me come up with a plan where I could do some self-care and ways they could help our family along with our "adoptive grandparents." That was God lifting me up through other people.

Ministry can be extremely rewarding, but it can also be hard. When I don't like church, it is because of several reasons:

- The lack of authentic relationships. Sometimes, it feels like there is a lot of pretending at church – like we all had it figured out. Well, I don't!

- The pressure of being the perfect wife, mom, and Bible Study Leader extraordinaire. I might be a pastor's wife, but I am a person facing the same struggles and challenges all women face. Some people find it uncomfortable when the pastors' wives admits to shortcomings.

- Doing it all. I have certain gifts and passions, but when I become the designated leader of whatever ministry needs to be filled, I minister outside of my gifting and I feel emotionally drained.

- People that don't like my husband or his choices. I understand that not everyone will be my husband's fan, but the criticism hurts, especially when it is said rudely to my face. Or when people make assumptions with no willingness to talk things through.

- The lack of support as a wife, mom, and special needs mom. Maybe we are supposed to have it all together – being a pastor's family – and maybe people assume we don't need help. We do.

- If I am not doing well emotionally or spiritually, it is difficult to attend church. I am a broken person with much need for grace and mercy like everyone else. I have a big and amazing God that carries me through these times and holds me in his arms while I wrestle, and question, and cry. You might not be a pastor's wife, but maybe you can identify with me. There is no perfect church, perfect family, or perfect people. So for now, I hold on to the promise that even through the hard times in ministry, God is good. And good doesn't mean easy, it means that God has it all figured out, and I need to trust in Him alone.

Reading this article helped me get a better understanding of what my wife goes through as a leading lady of our church. Not that I did not appreciate her already, it just made me appreciate her even more. I got a better understanding of the sacrifices she makes to support me in ministry and how she holds our family together while I'm doing "church stuff." One of the things I know now, that I did not realize at first, is that pastors' wives must have thick skin. They must be able to handle the constant criticism, unrealistic expectations, disrespect and lack of appreciation of them and their husbands/pastors. There are many impossible expectations that are placed on their shoulders.

Some church members are critical of pastor's wives because they do not participate in the ministries the members think they should. If that's not the case, the members get upset when they do not allow members into their personal space or get too close to their young children. Instead of allowing the pastors' wives to find their comfort zone and participate in the ministry they like or feel called to, they want to place them in charge of the Women's Ministry or the Deaconess Ministry. They expect them to dress and look a certain way. Some churches expect the pastor's wife to teach

Bible study and be as biblically sound as her husband. If they refuse to teach or if do not get involved in ministry like their husbands, then the members talk negative about them and call them "stuck up."

What some members do not understand is that pastors' wives are not called to be co-pastors; their job is to minister to their husbands and take care of their family. Some people may not like it, but if that is all they do then they have done their job and fulfilled their God-given assignment. Anything after that is a plus; and they should not be forced to serve on a ministry, or made to feel guilty if they choose not to do anything else. Taking care of the pastor/husband and their family is hard enough.

Understand this, when the pastors come home stressed and ready to quit, it's their wives who encourage them and gets them back on track. When they are doing too much and burning themselves out, it's the wives who make them sit down and rest so that they can be healthy enough to keep serving. While they are visiting the sick, marrying your loved one, burying your love ones, supporting your children's baby showers, graduations, football and basketball games, it's their wives who are home taking care of the family. The pastors' wives have a major ministry of their own. Although, it's not all done at church, they still play an important role for the church. Therefore, instead of judging and criticizing the pastors' wives, pray and thank God for them. This is especially true if you have good ones.

Being a pastors' wife is a tough responsibility. Below are a few suggestions on how you can assist your pastor's wife:

1. Pray for her
2. Support her as much as you can
3. Be a source of encouragement to her
4. Help her
5. Be a blessing to her
6. Don't judge her; try to better understand her
7. Let her know you are there for her
8. Protect her
9. Be a true friend to her
10. Love her

The pastors' wives have a very challenging and stressful job. With the help, prayers and assistance of some caring and understanding members, their job will be easier to manage. Also, churches should let your pastors' wives be themselves. It may take time for them to open up to you, but remember they have to share their husband and family with people they really do not know yet. Often times all they have in that city or church are their families and having to share them can be difficult. Therefore, when churches are showing love and kindness to the pastors, please do not forget their wives!

What About the Husbands of the Female Pastors

When writing this chapter, I wrote it out of my own experience and from a male's perspective. However, I do realize that there are many female pastors who have husbands. Being the husband of a female pastor does not mean there is a total role reversal, you are still in a supportive role to your spouse/pastor. While some of the spousal duties may differ as a male, the role of a pastor's husband is still essential to the success of the ministry and to their marriage. Just like the wives of pastors should be treated with respect and patience, so should the pastors' husbands. Contrary to popular belief, the pastors' husbands do not have to become deacons; especially if they are not called of God. Their number one priority is to take care of their wives and families.

There are many areas in the church where husbands can aid and support their wives' ministry other than the deacon board. They can be involved in the Christian Education Department if that's their desire or calling. They can be involved in communications, audio/visual, music, greeters, men's department and so much more. They should allow God to use and place them in areas that they feel lead, not an area to please members in the congregation. If the husbands feel God is calling them to be a deacon, they should be faithful to the call and serve with wholehearted devotion.

Husbands remember: you may be the head at home, but your wives are in charge at church. It is important to understand, you may be the head of your household, but you are not the pastor of the church. Therefore, husbands must be able to submit to their wives' authority and leadership; doing this will prevent any unnecessary drama for the wives and the families. The husbands must be the persons who keep their wives/pastors balanced and encouraged because ministry can be a burden. Similar to the male pastors needing their wives to be sources of strength, so do the female pastors need their husbands. When the husbands get frustrated and tired of dealing with church and "church folks," they must hang in there and do whatever it takes to support their wives.

Discussion Questions:

1. How can members make ministry a blessing for the pastors' spouses rather than a burden?

2. What are some unrealistic expectations for pastors' spouses?

3. Why do you feel some pastors' wives are very private and do not interact with a lot of people?

Chapter Six

PKs (Preachers' Kids) Get Hurt Too

Chapter Six

PKs (Preachers' Kids) Get Hurt Too

A FEW MONTHS AGO, I was sitting in my office thinking about the future of the church, and all the challenges we are facing trying to keep our churches full. While I was sitting there, I started thinking about my family and how they are affected as well. I started considering the challenges my children face being "the pastor/preacher's kids." When I began thinking about all they have to deal with literally put a tear in my eye. All these years pastoring, I never really took the time to look at ministry and church from their perspective. I always talked to them about what I go through as a pastor, but I never considered or even talked to them about what they go through as a preacher's kid or PK. It was at that moment I began to realize ministry not only brings challenges for the pastor and his/her spouse, it also creates challenges for the PKs.

Let me begin this section by stating that I am not a PK so I speak from secondhand knowledge. However, I have learned a lot of things about PKs talking to my own children and other PKs. I learned they get hurt too. I learned they suffer and have challenges at church just like their parents. One PK said, "People think the pastor and the first lady are the only ones who have a hard time at church, but we go through

101

stuff too." One of things that stuck with me was how many PKs feel like members place unfair expectations on them because of they are the pastors' or preachers' children. They felt like many church members expected them to be perfect or the best-behaved children in the church, when all they wanted was to be treated like all the other kids.

Placing these kinds of expectations on PKs is really unfair. Although they are a part of the first family, they are still human. They make mistakes just like all the other kids/young adults in the church. They like to have fun and turn up just like all the other kids. However, they feel pressure put on them by some people in the church to be that perfect child. One PK said he was ridiculed and talked about simply because he listened to rap music. Here is what was so unfair and unchristian about this particular situation: their children listen to rap music all the time. It was only a problem when the pastors' kids listened to it. In many cases, PKs are held to a higher standard. These high expectations are reasons why many PKs leave the church when they get of age.

I was also informed that many PKs are hurting and do not like the church because of the way their parents are treated. Many PKs see what some church members do not see, such as the sacrifices made for the church. PKs are usually the ones who are told "no" when their parents cannot attend an important event, game, recital, or something else because of obligations at church. Also, PKs are usually the ones who have to sacrifice family time because of the church.

Therefore, when they see their parent(s) being mistreated it makes them have negative feelings towards the church. I'm sure most pastors do not share all that they go through at church with their children. Yet, their children can see the pain in their faces or see the tears in their eyes. They know when their parents are going through tough times. I believe most PKs probably wish their parents would leave the church so that they can have a normal and peaceful life.

I read this letter from Barnabas Piper to future pastors teaching them what PKs would like them to know. I would like to share this letter with you because I believe it encompasses what many PKs feel. Here is what it says:

Dear Future Pastor,

> *You are called, or at least you're pretty sure you are. That's why you are heading into the great unknown called "vocational ministry." I understand that. I believe that. I believe God lays it on people's hearts in an undeniable way to serve His church as pastors. But you must know that this calling makes life difficult for your family, your children. While you feel the tractor beam of the pulpit, they don't. Your kids aren't called to ministry, and they don't want to challenge your calling either because that would mean challenging God. Neither, though, do they always like being the children of a minister. It can be difficult, but are they free to say so?*

Your calling casts a long and intimidating shadow, even if you don't.

You may think the challenges of being a pastor's kid (PK) are overstated. As one who spent my entire childhood, my college years, and my young professional and married life as a PK, I assure you they are not. You may be inclined to think you know what the challenges will be, but I suspect some are subtle enough as to have escaped your notice. The scrutiny, for example, is a subtle thing. Most people in your church will have good intentions and will be predisposed to like you and your family. All that liking means a whole lot of noticing, though. Parishioners will notice everything about your kids—bad habits, misbehaving in the supermarket, flirting, talking during service or Sunday school, running a stop sign, seeing an R-rated movie, who they're dating, who they just broke up with, and so forth.

Of course, you'll unwittingly encourage this by telling stories about your kids in your sermon too. No matter how kind people are, all that noticing piles on the pressure. It leaves no room for mistakes and erodes their sense of freedom. You are likely prepared for the double standard you will face as a pastor, the expectation to be morally flawless. Did you realize your kids will face the same? They will be expected to behave better, to believe better, to profess better, to lead better, to set an example. People will overlook the fact that by nature they're just like every other kid, and will expect something a tick more angelic. This is annoying at best, but it can have a devastating effect on your kids' identities and souls.

Will they define themselves by others' expectations? Will they base their worth on an extra-biblical moral standard? Will they be people pleasers or rebel against the expectations? Or might they hide their true selves, their questions, their fears and their doubts behind a faux moral façade just to survive, all the while not being sure what they actually believe. Will you be able to tell? Teaching is what you do. Each Sunday you will stand in front of a congregation and, if you're doing your job well, expound upon God's word, His character and His gospel. You will lead your family in devotions and have theological conversations. You will fill your kids with biblical truth as much as you can. The foundation of their faith will be laid and they will have a storage shed full of building blocks for belief. But will they know how to believe?

One of your greatest challenges will be discerning which answers your children give you are merely the "right" ones and which ones are truly windows to their souls. You will try to determine what they believe versus what they know they ought to believe. And the hard part is they often won't know the difference themselves. PKs are adept at giving the right answers and then giv-

ing the right answers to the follow-up questions. But answers and belief aren't the same thing. One is mental assent or mere mimicry. The other is a life changed from the inside out.

The scrutiny, the expectations, the double stand-ards and the lack of clarity about belief can create a witches brew of doubts and confusion. But to whom can PKs take their questions. Where is it safe? If they are expected to be "just so," to have the answers and to be more mature believers than their peers, then doubts and questions aren't OK. The church, where they ought to feel safest, becomes off limits. Even your job security will rest on their behavior and profession of faith. What are they to do? Will they view you as safe to confide in or will doing so be an assault on your calling?

Your children will need you to be their parent be-fore you are their pastor. Talk with them; don't preach at them. Listen to them as a confidant not a profes-sional counselor. When you can, protect them from the double standards heaped upon them. Your standing for them will be Supermanesque. While you won't always be able to protect them in public, be sure to make your home a haven of grace and consistency where you ad-mit your faults and ask forgiveness so they know they can do the same. And have fun with them. All your les-sons will pale in comparison to baseball, Barbies, Legos, fishing, biking, drawing or hiking. Enter into the hobbies they love and have a hobby you can fold them into so they feel part of your life. (Reading doesn't count; it's not a group activity.)

Be patient with your kids. They are kids, after all, just like all the other little delightful knuckleheads out there. They will hear you. They will know what you believe and what you stand for. They will absorb what you say, even if it doesn't show. Be patient and be present. Many PKs bloom late because it takes time to sort through the pressures and expectations to find their own identity and faith. They need your love, grace and prayers along the way. And they need to know that you don't care what expectations anyone else has for them. All you want is for them to live a life that pleases Jesus (The End).

After reading this letter and talking with my children it helped me get a better understanding of how they felt about church and ministry. I also informed them I was proud of them and they did not have to feel the pressure of being perfect because no one is perfect, not even me as the pastor. I shared with them the only expectation I have for them is to have a personal relationship with God and to be the best them they can be. I do not force them to work in ministry. I encourage them to use their gifts and talents to help me build God's church. One of my worst fears is that my children will grow up and not want to be a part of the church because of how they were treated; or because of what they have seen me go through at church. Nevertheless, I must realize PKs have their own struggles and challenges with ministry. There are times I have to be their father not just their pastor.

Here are a few things PKs need from their parents

    1) A parent, not a pastor

    2) Conversation, not sermons

    3) Your interest in their hobbies and activities

    4) Let them be themselves

    5) Consistency

    6) Grace to fail

    7) A single moral standard

    8) Unconditional love

    9) Family time

    10) Listen to them

Here are a few things PKs need from their church family
(This section is taken from an article written by Barnabas Piper on September 1, 2017)

3 Things Pastors' Kids Need from Their Churches

1) Let PKs be themselves.

For better and worse, let PKs be themselves. One of the hardest parts of being a PK is being what others expect you to be without ever being able to find out who you are. Remember how you came to faith? Remember how you've grown in faith? I bet it was through struggles, through mistakes, through seeing the profound grace of God when you needed it most. I bet it came when you connected with Jesus in the deeply personal way instead of trying to be perfect or live up to someone else's expectations. That's exactly what PKs need—the room to connect with Jesus like that. And it might be a winding road with mistakes along the way, in fact it probably will be. But that's OK.

2) Don't ask anything of a PK you wouldn't ask of anyone else.

One of the hardest things about being a PK is being known of by so many people you don't know. It's compounded when you interact as if you're friends even though they can't even remember your name. When you delve into their personal life, it doesn't feel like friends talking; it feels like an invasion of privacy. Even more so when you demand that they act a certain way. When seven boys are sprinting around the church lobby, why stop the PK? When all the high school girls are dressing a certain way, why call out the PK? Step back and realize that you might be unwittingly piling expectations and scrutiny on them even though your motives are pure.

109

3) Befriend them as a friend, not as a novelty.

PKs need friends they can trust, friends who care nothing about their last name and everything about their personhood. They need friends who will love them for who they are not because of their daddy's position in the church. They need friends who will help them, push them, listen to them and not judge them. These kinds of friends are the ones around whom PKs can begin to figure out who they really are, who God really is, and what it means to love Jesus in a personal way, not just a way that meets expectations.

Discussion Questions:

1. What are some other ways the church can hurt PKs?

2. How can the church help PKs love, and not grow to hate the church?

3. Do you feel the church members treat PKs differently? If so why?

4. If PKs had a bad experience and left the church, how can we get them back?

5. When correcting someone's wrong behavior, who would be the best person to approach that individual?

Chapter Seven

I Love My Church, But Sometimes "Church Folk" Get on My Nerves

Chapter Seven

I Love My Church, But Sometimes "Church Folk," Get on My Nerves

"Not everyone that saith unto me, Lord, Lord, shall enter into the kingdom of heaven... And then will I profess unto them, I never knew you: depart from me, ye that work iniquity."- Matthew 7:21, 23 (KJV)

WHEN SOMEONE states they have been hurt by the church or they have experienced "church hurt," what they are really saying is they have been hurt by an individual or a group of individuals in the church; not the building itself. Unfortunately, when situations like this occur, the church usually gets blamed. For example, when members are hurt or mistreated by another member, they not only get upset with the person who hurt them, they also have a tendency to leave the church. Although not always the case, those who leave make bad statements about the church. They say things like, "that church is no good" or "that church has too much drama." When statements like those are made, I consider it unfair to the church. You may have been hurt or mistreated by a member of the church, but it was not the entire church that hurt you.

If we're honest, most churches have members who mistreat other members and keep some form of drama going, but I do not believe the entire church is that way. One drama-filled member or a group of evil people do not make up the character or attitude of the entire church. Therefore, one bad person or one bad experience should not push you away and cause you to give up on the church. Neither should a bad experience with a member cause you to attach a negative label to the entire church. Everyone in the church is not bad. Yes, there are some mean-spirited members in every church; but, there are also many loving and caring members in every church. It is my prayer that in every church the good outweighs the bad.

Over the years, I have had my share of issues and bad experiences with people. I have experienced betrayal, been lied on, falsely accused, judged and taken advantage of, just to name a few. What may be shocking to some of you reading this is that most of those things I just mentioned did not happen to me when I was in the streets, they happened at church. Although somewhat sad to say, but the majority of the pain I have experienced in my adult years came from church or should I say "church folk." The very people who claimed they loved and served God. If you have been saved or a part of the church for at least three months, you probably can relate. I'm sure I do not have to tell you that "church folk" can be a trip. "Church folk" can be, as Paul says in 2 Corinthians 12:7, "A thorn in your flesh." They can make you want to leave church and never come back. Unfortunately, many churches are full of issues and are losing their members because of the behavior of some "church folk." That's

114

why I hear a lot people say they love the church, but "church folk" get on their nerves.

So that there is no confusion, when I say "church folk" I'm not referring to everyone that goes to church; I'm referring to the individuals that keep conflict and tension going on in the church. "Church folk" are those individuals who say they love their church, but are destroying the sanctity and unity within the church with their wicked ways. They do not come to church to worship; they come see what's going on in service so they can have something to gossip about later on. They also make it hard for others to enjoy worship because they keep so much stuff going on in church that it distracts from the worship experience. Every church, regardless of race or denomination, has some "church folk;" it's an unescapable reality.

I would like to suggest that every church has at least three groups of individuals in in the worship experience every Sunday morning: visitors, Christians and "church folk." In the event you did not know, there is a major difference between Christians and "church folk." It may be hard to tell the difference in the beginning because everyone looks the same when they are dressed up and looking holy in their Sunday best. You may also be confused because of their ability to quote a few scriptures and their outward expression of worship. But if you pay close attention to how everyone acts after service and how they treat other believers, you will clearly see the differences between the Christians and "church folk."

Here are a few distinctions:

"Church folk" give off a persona that they are perfect and have it all together; while, Christians know they are not perfect and still have a lot to work on.

"Church folk" are judgmental and extremely critical; while, Christians are compassionate and willing to help build others up.

"Church folk" cannot stand to see you get blessed, but Christians are happy for your success and the favor of God on your life.

"Church folk" will give large sums of money only so they can be viewed as big shots; while, Christians cheerfully give what they have no matter how much it is.

"Church folk" do everything out of selfish ambitions, but Christians do it from the heart.

"Church folk'" get mad if their names are not called for what they do, but Christians do not care if they get recognized as long as God gets the glory.

"Church folk" need titles and positions to validate them; Christians just want to be servants.

"Church folk" worry and fret about what they wear to church; while, Christians realize that what's on the inside is more important than what is on the outside.

116

"Church folk start problems; while, Christians do whatever it takes to solve problems.

"Church folk" claim to love everybody; Christians actually show love for everybody.

"Church folk" will gossip and talk bad about your issues; Christians will pray and help you get delivered and work through your issues.

"Church folk" will do you wrong and never apologize; while, Christians will admit their faults and try to make it right.

"Church folk" sit back and criticize everything, while Christians give solutions to make things better.

"Church folk" just attend church; while Christians are being changed, educated, and empowered by the church.

These are just a few distinct differences between Christians and "church folk," but the list can go on forever. It is my prayer that you are a fruit-bearing Christian helping to build the church and not one of those "church folk" causing havoc and running people away from the church. If for some reason you fall under the "church folk" category, it's not too late to make a change. Start with strengthening your relationship with Christ and make a serious commitment to grow spiritually. Also, stay humble and never get to the place where you think have arrived. This will keep you from being judgmental and overly critical of others who are not where you are spiritually.

My purpose in pointing out the differences between Christians and "church folk" is to show that although people may be in the same church, everyone does not have the same spiritual DNA. This is important to note because a person's spiritual DNA will determine how he or she will behave and treat other people. Many people have been hurt and disappointed by people in the church who look like Christians, but they had "church folk" DNA. I would go as far as to say that most of the pain and hurt that people have experienced in the church has been caused by "church folk," not Christians. "Church folk" have run more people away from the church than Satan. I know that may be hard to believe, but it's true. Satan does not care if we attend church; he simply does not want us to grow and be changed by the church. Satan does not care who becomes president of the ministry, whose names get called, what color we wear on our anniversary or who sings lead in the choir; only "church folk' care and fight over that kind of stuff. The reason Satan does not care about those things is because none of those things contribute to our spiritual growth and development. They actually hinder our growth more than they help our growth.

Moreover, Satan gets blamed for most of the challenges and drama that take place in the church. However, a lot of the issues we face have to do with the attitudes and behavior of "church folk." For example, "church folk" have selfish ambitions, egos, evil and jealous spirits, personal agendas, nasty attitudes and carnal minds. These things have been the cause for the majority of the problems that take place in church. Therefore, it's important that we develop a congregation of God-fearing Christians; not a congregation full of "church folk."

"Church Folk" Are Like the Scribes and Pharisees

In my opinion, Christians are like Jesus' disciples. Though not perfect people, they genuinely do their best to follow Christ and work on their flaws. On the other hand, "church folk" are more like the Pharisees and Scribes: religious, but not concerned about, or striving toward a better relationship with Christ. They have the religious thing down pat, but have little to no traits of the fruits of the spirit. They tend to hold people to a standard they themselves are not adhering to. Jesus calls people like that hypocrites (Matthew 23). Jesus instructed His listeners to respect the Scribes and Pharisees due to their position of authority, but not to emulate them because they did not practice what they preached. They tie up heavy, cumbersome loads and put them on other people's shoulders, but they themselves are not willing to lift a finger to move them. Everything they do is done for people to see (Matthew 23:3–5).

Furthermore, the Scribes and Pharisees were supposed to know God and help others know Him and follow His ways. Instead, these religious leaders added to God's Law, making it a cumbersome and onerous burden. They did not follow God with a pure heart. Their religion was not true worship of

God; rather it was rooted in a prideful heart. Therefore, Jesus called them hypocrites and bad examples to follow. Unfortunately, some people in the church have become just like the Pharisees and Scribes--religious, but bad examples to follow. They profess Christ, but their behavior does not emulate Him; we call them "church folk."

Modern Day Pharisees

When I was a young man in Sunday school, I heard countless stories and sermons about the Pharisees in the Bible; but I thought they were non-existent after Pentecost and the Christian movement began to flourish. However, when I started pastoring, I discovered that Pharisees, or the spirit of the Pharisees, still exist. Actually, most churches have some modern-day Pharisees. If you are wondering if you have modern-day Pharisees in your congregation this article written by Frank Powell entitled, *12 Signs You Are A Modern Day Pharisee*, should help answer that question.

12 signs you are a Modern-Day Pharisee

1.) **You believe showing up for worship every Sunday makes you right with God.**
   Modern-day Pharisees try to measure everything. They must have metrics and barometers. Something to measure their righteousness. Anything to give them some security with God. And I am not against barometers or metrics. Not at all. Barometers can reveal trends and expose inconsistencies. But modern-day Pharisees see metrics as essen-

tial to righteousness and salvation. Worship is not a time to draw into God. Worship is another check off the list. For modern-day Pharisees, Christian living is not so much about transforming into the image of God. It is more about living up to the standard of God. And no one can live up to God's standard. Except Jesus.

2.) You spend more time talking about what you are against, not what you are for.

Pharisees love to argue. They love to spend their time convincing others. If they had to list the actions and issues they are against, the pencil would run out of lead. But turn around and ask them to list what they are for? The pencil would not have to be re-sharpened. Pharisees believe their job is to defend God and legislate morality. So they are against drinking, smoking, cursing, short skirts, talking back to parents, holding hands before marriage, and so on. And all of these things come before the gospel. Or maybe they are the gospel. Modern-day Pharisees can't tell the difference.

3.) You believe God actually needs you.

Modern-day Pharisees believe God needs them on His team. They believe the church is dependent upon them. Let me be real with the modern-day Pharisees. If God needs a human being for His church to survive, He is not a God worth serving. Or worshipping. Or following. God needs no one. God simply allows us to play a role. He allows us to play a part. If God needs a human being for His church to survive, He is not a God worth serving.

121

4.) You don't repent of sin...you don't have any "serious" sin to repent of.

Remember that time the modern-day Pharisees repented of sin in their life? Oh wait, they never have. They don't have any serious sin to repent of. Pharisees have a reputation and status to maintain. Repentance involves vulnerability and weakness. Pharisees don't show weakness. Who cares if the God of the universe was humiliated and mocked by mere men? That has no bearing on a modern-day Pharisee. Repentance is for people who sin really bad. Not for them.

5.) You make every issue black and white.

The Bible is grey on many issues. But modern-day Pharisees don't deal in the world of grey. They must have everything black and white. In or out. Yes or no. Up or down. You see, if an issue is grey, modern-day Pharisees have to do some work on the heart. And Pharisees don't work on the heart. They don't consider motives. Here is another thing about grey. It does not allow modern-day Pharisees to keep score. Black and white issues, however, allow them to keep a tally of their righteousness. "I have never drank or smoke or gambled or cheated on my wife." Who cares if their heart is full of lust, anger, and envy? Making a grey issue black and white means modern-day Pharisees don't have to deal with the motives underneath their actions.

6.) You would never condone homosexuality or fornication...but have no problem watching movies that do.

If someone were to preach on the evils of homosexuality or sex before marriage, a modern-day
Pharisee would nod his or her head in agreement.
"Yeah, that's right preacher. Preach on!" But on
Sunday night, they plop down in the recliner and
find humor from a movie or TV show glamorizing
the very thing they just agreed was wrong. This is
the real issue with modern-day Pharisees. They
love to put on a show when the lights are on. They
want people to think they are righteous. But Jesus
does not inform the rest of their lives. After all,
they went to church...and life group. The checklist
is complete.

7.) Your salvation is based on your works, not on Jesus.

Modern-day Pharisees believe in their works.
That's why they love James 2:14-26. But they skirt
around passages about grace. Oh, yeah. They believe Jesus died on the cross for their sins. But they
turn around and mock the cross by trying to earn
their salvation.

8.) You read the Bible to substantiate your convic-tions, not to be shaped into God's image.

During the time of Jesus, no one knew more Scripture than the Pharisees. They studied the
Scriptures relentlessly. Modern-day Pharisees do
the same. But they turn around and use the
knowledge to convince others why they are
wrong. The Bible is their personal weapon. Modern-day Pharisees use it to throw rocks at all the
misguided, evil sinners in the world. To modern-
day Pharisees, the Bible is not a means to grow in-

to the image of God. It is a means to convince the world of fallacies and misguided theology.

9.) You believe outsiders should conform to a certain lifestyle before they are accepted as "Christian."

This is a Pharisee trademark. Before non-Christians can be considered "part of the group," they must conform to a certain lifestyle. Stop all of the cursing and drinking. And stop doing all the stuff "bad people" do. Once potential Christians "fix their lives," modern-day Pharisees gladly welcome these people into their family. Just don't revert back to "sinning" again. Membership in the group is always conditional. Instead of meeting people where they are, modern-day Pharisees force people to come up to their level.

10.) You don't know the difference between a convert and a transfer.

Modern-day Pharisees get just as excited when someone joins their church as they do when someone joins the kingdom of God. In fact, they don't see much distinction between the two. They celebrate a baptism the same way they celebrate a family moving from across the street. This is why no real desire for the lost exists. The church is adding "members." But they are being added to the directory of the local church, not the directory of the Kingdom. Modern-day Pharisees don't care. As long as the "church" is adding people.

11.) All of your Christian friends look and act just like you do.

124

Pharisees are exclusive. They pick and choose who enters the group. But Jesus never valued exclusivity. Just look at his chosen twelve. A tax collector (Matthew). A doctor (Luke). Fishermen (Peter and Andrew). A Zealot (Simon). That's a conglomerate of guys from many different backgrounds. So, look around at your group? Is it essentially a collection of men and women cut from the same mold?

12.) If someone tries to rebuke you, you get angry and offended.

Remember what happened Jesus rebuked the Pharisees? Their hearts broke. They repented. And Jesus used them to start the church. When Jesus called out their sins, the Pharisees crucified him. Modern-day Pharisees see any rebuke as a personal attack. They immediately go on the offensive. Some get angry and storm off. Others proceed to make a list of sins to the person rebuking them. Regardless, modern-day Pharisees refuse to have a heart receptive to rebuke. It undermines their external righteousness.

Conclusion

All over the world, churches are declining and people are leaving in record number. This mass exodus from the church has caused many congregations to suffer and struggle just to survive. There are many reasons why people leave churches, but one of the major reasons why so many are leaving is because of "church hurt." They have been hurt or mistreated by someone in the church. As previously mentioned, most of the pain and hurt inflicted upon someone in the church was caused by "church folk" who can also be considered modern-day Pharisees. If you talk with individuals who left the church due to "church hurt," the majority of them would probably say, I love God and my church, but "church folk" get on my nerves.

Discussion Questions:

1. Have you ever had a bad encounter with "church folk?" Did it make you want to leave the church? If so why?

2. What impact have "church folk" had on your church?

3. How can we stop "church folk" or Modern-day Pharisees from running members away from our churches?

4. What can you do to ensure you do not become like "church folk" or Modern-day Pharisees?

Chapter Eight

"Church Folk" Are Too Judgmental

Chapter Eight

"Church Folk" Are Too Judgmental

If any of you is without sin, let him be the first to throw a stone.
John 8:7(NIV)

"You hypocrite, first take the plank out of your own eye, and then
you will see clearly to remove the speck from your brother's eye."
Matthew 7:5 (NIV)

WHEN I BEGAN the process of writing my second book, "Changing the Way We Do Church," I interviewed approximately fifty people regarding why they no longer attended church. There were multiple reasons given such as work, their children had activities on Sunday mornings, relocated, or displeasure with pastor and/or the preaching. One lady stated she does not attend because it's her only day off. However, the one reason mentioned most consistently was: too much "drama and mess" in the church. When I asked them to clarify what exactly this meant, some stated "people are phony and they treat you like you don't belong." Another person said, "I left because 'church folk' are too judgmental; they judged me and they didn't even know me."

When I heard one person claim he left because church folk were too judgmental, I was not shocked because I somewhat agree with that statement. Whether we want to face reality or not, there are too many critical and judgmental people in our churches. Unfortunately, some of the most judgmental people you will ever meet will not be on your job, school, or in your neighborhood, they will be sitting right up in the church. These individuals shout, quote scriptures and act spiritual. It's a sad reality, but some people came to church, got saved, and then develop a case of amnesia. They acquired a title, learned a few bible verses, and proceeded to act like they forgot from where they came. They deemed themselves faultless and better than everyone else.

In addition, some "church folk" will talk about you and your issues as if they never did anything wrong or never had any issues themselves. It is these "super saints/church folk" who are creating an unhealthy church culture and turning people away from the church. This is puzzling to me because none of us are perfect and all of us are an "ex" something. I realize some of us have more ex's than others, but we all have a past and have done things of which we are not proud. All of us have engaged in some activities we are keeping between God and ourselves. No, I'm not just referring to before we got saved, for even after we became saved we still messed up and let God down.

Regrettably, countless people have been mistreated and ridiculed because they came to church with their issues, or someone in the church discovered their issues. Instead of receiving help and compassion from members, they were unfairly judged and treated as if they did not belong. I personally know of a few individuals who have not only been judged by the church, they been ousted due to members not agreeing with their sexual orientation. A same sex couple was told they had to leave and find somewhere else to worship because that church did not condone same sex marriage. They would not tolerate that type of behavior. Situations such as these are pushing people away from the church, causing those who attend to hide their issues in fear of being judged and mistreated.

However, treating people like this is contrary for what God's church stands. All are welcomed in God's house regardless of personal proclivities and issues. It is often said the church is a hospital for the sick. However, some people in the church act as if they do not want flawed people to attend. When this happens, they make the church hypocritical; becoming the only hospital that does not want sick patients. Many people go to church to get help with their issues, not to be judged and ill-treated because of their issues. The church should be a place of compassion, not a courtroom convicting people without giving them a fair trial. Instead of judging each other, we should show love and compassion towards each other. Remember, we all have flaws and things we need to work on.

This is the message Jesus taught to his disciples and the crowd in Matthew, Chapter 7. Reading this chapter you will discover it is the concluding portion of Jesus' "Sermon on the Mount." In this sermon, Jesus lays out for His hearers how to live a spiritually mature life fit for God's kingdom. He begins the sermon with what many scholars refer to as the Beatitudes. If you ever want to know how your attitude should be, just read the Beatitudes. In addition, if you desire a reference of how to treat each other, even our enemies, read the Beatitudes.

In the "Sermon on the Mount," Jesus taught his hearers how their attitudes should be regarding giving, praying, fasting, and dealing with difficult people. He urged them to follow the proper way to live and represent God's kingdom. Jesus had to teach them the right way to live due to the Pharisees and Scribes setting poor examples. Oddly enough, although the Pharisees and Scribes were very religious people, they still had a major issue, self-righteousness. They were pious and somewhat sanctimonious. For some reason, the Pharisees and Scribes believed they were the standard. In their minds, they should be the ones revered because they possessed high positions and respectable titles. However, what they failed to misunderstand, neither their titles nor positions made them perfect or more acceptable to God. Their positions and titles did not guarantee they had it all together.

Here is something many believers and frequent churchgoers need to understand today: a title or position in the church does not mean you have arrived. It does not deem you are holy and acceptable to God. Some of the worldliest people you will ever meet have titles and positions. Your titles and positions do not make you divine; they simply mean you have more responsibility than others. Therefore, a person's attitude and humility should not change just because he or she has been elevated and given a title. When you have been elevated or chosen to serve in any capacity, your humility and compassion for others should increase.

One of the major issues the Pharisees and Scribes had was how they believed themselves to be of high prominence. They were so self-righteous; they placed themselves above everybody else and looked down on anyone who was not on their level. That was one of the primary reasons Jesus called them hypocrites. Even though they had titles and positions, they were no better than anyone else. Nothing was right in their eyes; they believed everybody had issues, except them.

Let's be frank, there are some Pharisees and Scribes in all of our churches who believe they have it all together and have a right to judge everybody else. We all have some people with pharisaic proclivities. The ones who have the tendency to look down on other people and criticize everything they do as if they are the only ones living in this world without sin. But the last time I checked, the Bible states in Romans 3:23 that "All have sinned and fall short of the glory of God." None of us are perfect and we all have sin and issues in our lives. With that said, no one has the right to look down on another person with a judgmental and superior spirit. We may not have the same sin, but we all have sin. It does not matter how one perceives or tries to justify it, to God sin is sin.

Therefore, given that we are all flawed, we should leave the judging to the Lord. This was the point Jesus was trying to teach his disciples and other hearers; Let God be the judge. If you judge you will be judged. He says "For in the same way you judge others you will be judged, and with the same measure you use, it will be measured to you" (Matthew 7:2).

Now the challenge with this text is so many people misunderstand what Jesus meant when He said, "Do not judge." This has caused a number of people to take this scripture out of context, thinking it means all judging is wrong. Some people have gone so far as to say we should not have judges in the court of law because the Bible commands, do not judge.

However, that's not what Jesus meant when He said, "Do not judge" (Matthew 7:1). Jesus is not saying we should ignore all wrong behavior; neither is He forbidding us from distinguishing or taking a stand between right and wrong. We have to be able to discern what's right and what's wrong in order to please God. In fact, throughout the Bible we are commanded to discern and to try the spirit by the spirit (1John 4:1). When Jesus says "do not judge," He's talking about blind, ignorant, hypocritical, self-righteous judging that overlooks one's own faults, failures and flaws, and only sees faults, failures and flaws in other people. He's talking about criticizing and condemning someone because of their issues as if you do not have any issues of your own.

There are a few reasons in Matthew, Chapter 7, why Jesus instructs us not to judge. The first being, they were not qualified to judge. Jesus wanted them as well as all of us to know that only God is qualified to judge. We can evaluate and discern, but we are not qualified to condemn. When we start condemning people, we put ourselves in the place of God. It should go without saying that it's dangerous to put yourself in God's place. Remember, the last time an individual tried to put himself in God's place he got kicked out of heaven. If you don't believe me, just ask Lucifer!

God does not have an issue with us having a constructive evaluation of an individual or situation, the problem is the manner in which we evaluate. When we start condemning people and passing final judgment on people, that's when it becomes a problem. Also, when we start convicting people and labeling them, it becomes a problem. Whether or not we agree with their behavior, judgment belongs to God alone. I know some people may disagree with me due to being long-time church members and they feel qualified to judge; but if you did not die on the cross and get up on the third day, you are not qualified. Judgment belongs to God!

Yet another reason Jesus states we should not judge is because our ability to judge correctly is flawed. Even if He gave us the chance to judge, we would still be unable to judge correctly due to our limited perception. Consider this question: in Matthew 7:4 Jesus asks, and I paraphrase, "how can you see a speck of saw dust in your brother's eye when you have a lumber yard or a piece of plywood in your own eye?"

This is His attempt to demonstrate to His followers how limited our perception is due to our own biases. The only way to see someone else's issues is to ignore and look past what's wrong with you; focusing on what's wrong with someone else. This is what the Bible considers a hypocrite. We cannot help anyone get delivered from hypocrisy. Each person must work on fixing his or her own problems before attempting to fix somebody else's problems.

Further along in the Chapter, Jesus offers a final reason why we should not judge. It primarily stems from the fact that we are incapable of making a fair, unbiased assessment on what someone has done if we do not know why he or she did it. We cannot judge a person's behavior if we do not know the motive behind his or her behavior. Also, just because you know a few things about a person does not mean you truly know that person. Therefore, if you don't know why someone did what he or she did, you definitely should not judge them for past or even current behavior. Simply, you should never judge a person's decisions when you have no knowledge of his or her options. Sadly, people have a tendency of judging your decisions, but they have no idea of your options. Yet somehow, they always have something to say. In my opinion, the world and the church would be better places if everyone would just work on themselves and not spend all their time judging and trying to fix everyone else. If this happens, instead of people leaving the church, they probably will feel comfortable enough to come to church and seek help and guidance from other believers.

How Should We Respond to Those Who Have Issues

All of us at some point in time will encounter someone who has sinned or has some visible issues in their lives. We are not to judge or condemn, what should be our response? There are many ways we can respond, but I believe Jesus gives us a great example of how we should respond in John Chapter 8 when the woman was caught in the act of adultery. The bible lets us know that the men who caught the woman in adultery brought her to Jesus because they wanted to see if Jesus was going to condemn her and sentence her to death according to the Law of Moses. Jesus being God in the flesh could have condemned her due to her sinful behavior. However, He did not condemn her; rather He gave her compassion and challenged her to live better. They figured Jesus would judge her, but Jesus said, he who is without sin throw the first stone. Given that they had all sinned, none of them could condemn her. The Bible says, they all walked away starting with the older ones first until only Jesus and the woman were left. When they all left, Jesus asked her where her persecutors were. He also asked if anyone condemned her. She said, no. Jesus said, "Neither, do I condemn you, but go and sin no more (John 8:7-9)."

137

Jesus did not condone or accept her sin, but He gave her compassion and challenged her to leave her life of sin. This is a great example for all us to follow when it comes to dealing with people who are struggling with sin in certain areas of their lives. We do not have to agree with that person's sin or lifestyle, but we should treat him or her with love and compassion. We can also help them to live better and correct some of their sinful behaviors without being judgmental. Let's never forget that despite all of our sin, God gave us grace. Consequently, we should be willing to do the same for somebody else. You may have overcome your sin quickly; others may not be able to overcome theirs quickly. Even if it takes a little longer than you would like; be prayerful, not judgmental.

Discussion Questions:

1. Why do you think people are so judgmental?

2. How can you disagree with a person's lifestyle without being offensive and judgmental?

3. What should you do if someone is wearing something in church that you feel is inappropriate?

4. What's the difference between constructive criticism and being judgmental?

5. When correcting someone's wrong behavior who would be the best person to approach that individual?

Chapter Nine

Let It Go So That You Can Move on With Your Life

Chapter Nine

Let It Go So That You Can Move on With Your Life

*"Get rid of all bitterness, rage and anger, brawling and slander,
along with every form of malice. Be kind and compassionate to one
another, forgiving each other, just as in Christ God forgave you."*
(Ephesians 4:31-32)

IN THE INTRODUCTION OF THIS BOOK, I shared a small portion of my story about the "church hurt" I experienced after accepting my call to ministry. I remember it like it was yesterday. Without a doubt, it was one of the most painful and discouraging seasons of my ministry. I thank God I was able to put it all behind me and move on with my life and ministry. Now, I am at a place in my life where I can look back on that experience and say what Joseph said to his brothers in Genesis 50:20, "You intended to harm me, but God intended it for my good to accomplish what is now being done, the saving of many lives." The reason I feel that way is because everything that happened to me at that church helped me get to where I am now. Yes, it hurt me; but, it also helped me grow.

Although I am at a place of peace now, it took me a long time to get to this state of mind. After I went through that particular situation, I was not only hurt and disappointed; I was also angry and bitter. My feelings were so negative towards that church that I left and joined another church. However, leaving one church and joining another one did not give me the peace I needed, nor did it heal my pain. For years, I held a grudge against some of the people in that church because of how I was treated. It was not until I truly let it go and moved on did I gain internal peace. Not only did I receive peace, I also fell in love with ministry again. It was at that point that my ministry took off and new doors started opening.

Taking advantage of the new doors and opportunities was the easy part, the hard part was letting go of the anger and moving on. To be honest, in the beginning I wanted to get even. I wanted them to feel the pain and devastation I felt when they hurt me. When I first left that church, I was so angry I started hoping the membership would fall off and they would suffer financially. I wanted bad things to happen to that church. Then I remembered the entire church did not hurt me, only a few people. As I mentioned in one of the earlier chapters, the whole church should not suffer or be penalized because of the actions of a few. Although a few people wronged me, overall, there were many loving and caring people in that church; a number of whom I still care about today. However, my anger with some of the people made me take out my frustration on the entire church. This often happens when people are hurt by individuals in the church, they usually make the same mistake I made — blaming the whole church.

Furthermore, when I finally left the church, a lot of people were shocked and confused. During the time I was going through my situation, I never mentioned it to anyone. But once I left the church, I shared everything with family and close friends. I also did something I would later regret. When people asked why I left, I told them my story and I also talked badly about the church. I grew to regret it because painting a bad picture of the church was not the right thing to do, especially when it was not a bad church. That church was the catalyst for changing my life and making me a better man. It was also responsible for getting my family back in church. Therefore, I should not have allowed one bad incident to overshadow all the good that took place in that church. It is my prayer that if anyone leaves a church due to some form of "church hurt," he or she will not allow the bad to overshadow the good. Remember, when you tell all the bad things that happened, please do not forget to tell all the good also.

Forgiveness is the First Step of Letting Go and Moving on

Thinking back to those days after I went through my situation of "church hurt," I realized I held onto that grudge for a long time. Although I did not talk much about the church or the people in the church, I still had negative feelings towards many of them. It was not until I attended a Bible study class my pastor taught on forgiveness that I forgave. At the class, I was convicted and challenged to let go and move on. During this particular class, we were talking about how Jesus forgave His persecutors while He was hanging on the cross. It amazed me that after all they did to Him on that Good Friday, Jesus still asked His Father to forgive them (Luke 23:34). When I read this passage of scripture, I said if Jesus can forgive the people who were crucifying Him, who am I not to forgive the people who treated me wrong. I also realized if I was going to be right with God, I needed to forgive and let some stuff go.

This was a major challenge for me, largely because in order for me to do the right thing, I had to forgive the people who hurt me even though they never apologized or showed any remorse for what they did. Forgiving someone is hard in itself. Yet, it's even harder to forgive people when they act unbothered or they do not show any sense of remorse or regret for what was done. I have learned not everyone will apologize or regret what they did to you. Some people truly do not care. Regardless of how the person(s) act who hurt you, we are still commanded by God to forgive (Colossians 3:13).

We must all understand that forgiveness is a deliberate decision to release your feelings of resentment or vengeance toward a person or group of individuals who hurt you; regardless of whether they actually deserve it. Therefore, extending forgiveness is not based on the person who hurt you apologizing or correcting what they did wrong; it's based on your obedience to God's Word.

Furthermore, even if they do not say sorry or acknowledge their fault, we still have to forgive them and move on. It may not seem fair, but as Christians who are trying to be more like Christ, it's the right thing to do. Bear in mind when you forgive someone, you're not doing it for them; you are actually doing it for yourself. You are forgiving them so that you can move on and have peace in your life. Therefore, if you are still holding a grudge against a person or a group of individuals who hurt you, start your season of peace today and forgive!

Here are a few scriptures on forgiveness that will help us understand what God requires as it relates to forgiveness and forgiving others:

- Be kind and compassionate to one another, forgiving each other, just as in Christ God forgave you (Ephesians 4:32).

- For if you forgive other people when they sin against you, your heavenly Father will also forgive you (Matthew 6:14).

- Bear with each other and forgive one another if any of you has a grievance against someone. Forgive as the Lord forgave you (Colossians 3:13).

- Do not judge, and you will not be judged. Do not condemn, and you will not be condemned. Forgive, and you will be forgiven (Luke 6:37).

145

- And when you stand praying, if you hold anything against anyone, forgive them, so that your Father in heaven may forgive you your sins (Mark 11:25).

- Then Peter came up and said to him, "Lord, how often will my brother sin against me, and I forgive him? As many as seven times?" Jesus said to him, "I do not say to you seven times, but seventy-seven times (Matthew 18:21-22).

- So watch yourselves. "If your brother or sister sins against you, rebuke them; and if they repent, forgive them. Even if they sin against you seven times in a day and seven times come back to you saying 'I repent,' you must forgive them" (Luke 17:3-4).

A Biblical Example of Forgiveness

The story of Joseph, in the book of Genesis is a prime example of a person extending forgiveness to the individuals who hurt him. It is one of my favorite stories in the whole Bible because we can learn many valuable life lessons from Joseph. One of the most important lessons we can learn from this story is you can overcome the obstacles in your life by remaining faithful to God. No matter what obstacles you face, you can overcome by remaining faithful to God. Joseph went through some major trials in his life, but he came out on top because he remained faithful to God. He did not allow his trials or unfortunate situations to separate him from God. Regardless of what he went through with his brothers or while in slavery, Joseph remained faithful to God. This story is proof that when you are faithful to God, He will be faithful to you.

When you read the fourteen chapters of Genesis 37-50, you will discover this story is really a handbook of how to deal with the challenges and drama of everyday life. Joseph's life was filled with problems, frustration, tailored with temptation, flooded with favor, linked with love and saturated with salvation. Joseph went through a lot of drama all because he had favor and God called him for a greater purpose. Still another message we learn from this story is while favor is great to have, it comes with various types of problems. I know a lot of people desire/seek favor, but the question they need to ask themselves is: can I handle all the drama and problems that comes with it? Hence, before you pray and ask God for favor, make sure you are ready to deal with all that comes with it. Having favor in your life is a blessing, but it can also be a burden. Joseph will tell you first hand that having favor was a blessing, but it came with some major burdens.

For Joseph, initially life was smooth sailing. He simply enjoyed being one of the younger brothers growing up in his father's house. However, things started changing for him once he began receiving favor. Out of all of Jacob's sons, Joseph was his favorite. He loved him more than all of the rest. To signify his love and favoritism for Joseph, Jacob gave him a coat of many colors. I'm sure Joseph was overjoyed to receive this coat. However, what he did not realize was how much his brothers would despise him because of the coat. The coat Jacob gave Joseph represented purity, position and privilege. In short, Jacob let everyone know, especially his other sons, his intentions to treat Joseph as his firstborn son. Consequently, his brothers started hating him because they felt he was receiving stuff he really did not deserve.

Still, that was not the only reason they hated Joseph, his brothers also hated him because of his dreams. Joseph had a dream that one day everyone, including his brothers, was going to bow down to his feet. Although the dream was true, Joseph made the big mistake of sharing his dream with his brothers. The Bible tells us when his brothers heard the dream, they became even more incensed and decided to kill Joseph. Another gem we can glean from Joseph's story is you have to be very careful with whom you share your dreams. You cannot share everything God shows you with every-body, because some people cannot handle it. Not everyone will be excited about what God is getting ready to do in your life. Some people will be very jealous and will do anything they can to stop it.

That is exactly what happened in this story. Joseph's brothers heard him tell his dream and it made them hate him even more. It was so bad that they were determined to get rid of him. One day Jacob sent Joseph to check on his brothers. When they saw him coming from a distance, they decided this was their chance to kill Joseph and put an end to all the favoritism and dreaming foolishness. They were going to eliminate him and his dream. His brothers, nonetheless, did not understand that when God gives you a dream nobody can kill you before it comes to pass. When God puts a vision down in your soul or has a plan for your life, you cannot die until it has been manifested. Therefore, you do not have to waste time fighting people who are trying to stop you or hinder what God is planning to do through you. People do not have the power or authority to stop what God has planned for your life. If God said it, it shall come to pass, and no devil in hell, on earth, or in church can stop it.

The story goes on to say that when Joseph came to where his brothers were, they stripped him out of his coat. Instead of killing him right away, they threw him in a pit. As they were sat eating and discussing how they were going to get rid of him, Judah saw the Ishmaelite's coming. They sold Joseph as a slave. While enslaved, Joseph ended up in Potiphar's house as a servant where he would later be falsely accused by Potiphar's wife. This led to him being thrown into prison for something he did not do. However, Joseph was released from prison and brought to the palace. There, he helped the Pharaoh of Egypt interpret his dreams. Due to the favor on his life, Joseph was elevated to the second highest position in the entire land of Egypt.

When Joseph interpreted Pharaoh's dreams, he told him a severe famine would come and they needed to prepare for it. Thank God Pharaoh listened to Joseph because the famine came all over the face of the Earth, just as Joseph predicted. It was such a severe famine that almost everyone was without food and the essentials that they needed to survive. Although everyone in the land suffered due to the famine, the people of Egypt were able to maintain because Joseph stored food before the famine came. People from across the world had to come to Joseph, in Egypt, to buy what they needed to survive.

When Jacob heard that they had corn in Egypt, he sent his sons to go get what they needed to survive. This is where the story gets good! When Jacob's sons got down to Egypt, they did not know it was Joseph; but they bowed down to his feet begging him to sell them what they needed to survive. How ironic, the same person they had hated and wanted to kill was the very one they ended up needing to help them survive. This is one of the reasons why we have to be careful how we treat people, because we never know when we might need them again. Please take this seriously because you never know when you going to need a person's help to get you out of a tough situation. The person you are hating and talking bad about could be the same person you will later need to bless you.

Joseph's brothers ended up needing the assistance of the same person they hated and thought they got rid of. What I found interesting was they did not recognize Him. Joseph knew who they were, but they did not know who Joseph was. They did not know it was their brother until he re-

150

vealed himself to them. In Chapter 45, verse 1, the Bible says, Joseph could no longer control himself so he cleared the room, and he "made himself known to his brothers." Joseph now stood before the same people who hurt him, tried to kill him and sold him into slavery. What's so powerful about this story is Joseph did not do what I assumed he was going to do to his brothers. Neither, did he do what you probably would have done. Joseph did what God desires for all of us to do to the people who have hurt, lied, betrayed or did something to us we did not like; he extended forgiveness. He forgave his brothers and aided them in their time of need.

That's exactly what God expects us to do. Regardless of what someone has done to you, forgive them and move on with your life. I can hear you through the pages of this book saying, you do not know what I have been through. You do not know what I had to go through as a result of what that person did to me. I hear you saying, how can I forgive someone whom tried to kill me, or murdered someone I loved? How can I forgive someone who has touched me in a way they were not supposed to? How can I forgive someone who has raped me and physically abused me? How can I forgive someone who participated in giving birth to me, but did not participate in raising me? How can I forgive someone who cheated on me and betrayed my trust? How can I forgive someone who stole from me? How can I forgive someone who touched my child in the wrong way? How can I forgive when I still feel pain?

I wish I could give you all the right answers to those questions; but, honestly, I cannot. I wish I could give you the right prayers, the right sermons, or the right books to read that will convict you and put you in the mental place to forgive. I wish I could give you what you need to make you get beyond what happened to you so that you can forgive and move on with your life. Sorry, only God can do that. Therefore, I cannot tell you how to motivate yourself to forgive. I can only tell you why you have to forgive.

After reading all that happened to Joseph as a result of what his brothers did to him, I wanted to know what made him forgive them. What made him look beyond what they did and not only forgive them, but help them in their time of need? Unfortunately, I was unable to speak to Joseph directly; but in my meditation, Joseph spoke to me through the text. He said it was hard to forgive, but I had to forgive because it was the right thing to do.

When God first gave Joseph the dream, he was prideful and started bragging about what God was doing in his life. We all know God hates pride. The Bible says, in Proverbs 16:5, "The Lord detests all the proud of heart. Be sure of this: They will not go unpunished." Joseph was prideful about his dream. When he was boasting about his dream, God could have stripped it away and let his brothers kill him. However, God forgave him and blessed him in spite of his issues. Therefore, Joseph said, I had to forgive them for what they did because God forgave me for what I did. It's the right thing to do. If God has forgiven you for what you have done to Him, you should be able to forgive someone else for what they did to you.

Moreover, Joseph also forgave his brothers because he realized it was the only way he could bring closure to his past. I believe Joseph forgave them because he desired to bring his pain to an end. Forgiveness is the only way of releasing ourselves from the pain we have experienced at the hands of others. Forgiveness does not mean you agree with what the other person did to you, it just means you are tired of bearing it and are ready to move on with your life. Sadly, a lot of people do not have any peace and cannot move on with their lives because they are still holding onto a grudge about something that happened a long time ago. That is not a good place to be for anyone. You have to pray and let go of some stuff. You must let the Holy Spirit remove the bitterness from your heart; freeing you to move on with your life.

Letting go is important because God has so much in store for you in the future. You will end up missing it if you do not let some stuff go. I know they hurt you and what they did was not right, but you still have to let it go. This is the hard part: whether they say sorry or not you still have to forgive and let it go. It is the only way you will be able to bring closure to your past and move on with your life. Joseph understood this principle and that's why he was willing to forgive his brothers.

This point is made clear in Genesis, Chapter 41. The Bible lets us know that Joseph had two sons, one named Manasseh and the other named Ephraim. In biblical times, names had significance. Every name had a meaning attached to it. Sometimes people named their child based on their (*sitz em labin*) situation in life. For instance, Joseph named his children based on his situation in life. Manasseh's name means "the Lord has caused me to forget all of my troubles." Ephraim's name means "the Lord has caused me to be fruitful." He named his first son Manasseh because God caused him to be forgetful. He named his second son Ephraim because the Lord caused him to be fruitful. Joseph said that before he could become fruitful, he first had to be forgetful. Meaning, he gave birth to forgiveness before he became fruitful in life. The lesson we can learn from Joseph is, before God blesses us to be fruitful, we have to forgive and put some stuff behind us.

But wait, there is a final reason I believe Joseph forgave his brothers. I believe he forgave them because when he spiritually processed the whole situation, he realized they actually helped him. His brothers thought they were hurting him, but they actually helped him to fulfill his God-given purpose. Joseph said to his brothers in Chapter 45:5 "Don't be distressed or angry with yourselves for selling me here, because it was to save lives that God sent me here." Joseph realized that his brothers sent him to be a slave, but God sent him to be a savior. All the brothers actually did was put him in position to receive what God had for him. Joseph looked at his brothers and said I'm not mad at you. I ended up right where I said I would be and you are the ones who helped me get here. When you spiritually process the whole situation of your life, you will realize that the people who thought they were hurting you actually helped you. Therefore, there is no need to harbor hatred for the person(s) who hurt you because God took what he or she did to you and made it work for your good. The best thing you can do for yourself is forgive them; then, move on with your life!

Discussion Questions:

1. Do you find it hard to forgive someone who has hurt you? If so, why?

2. How does holding on to a grudge make you feel? Has it helped you or made the situation even more difficult?

3. After you forgave someone how did that make you feel? Did you have more peace?

4. How does not forgiving a person hurt you more than it hurts the person you are angry with?

Chapter Ten

Forgiveness Has No Limits

Chapter Ten

Forgiveness Has No Limits

Then Peter came to Jesus and asked, "Lord, how many times shall I forgive my brother or sister who sins against me? Up to seven times?" Jesus answered, "I tell you, not seven times, but seventy-seven times." (Matthew 18:21, 22)

IN THE PREVIOUS CHAPTER, I talked about the need to forgive the people who have done you wrong so you can have peace and can move on with your life. Although most Christians know we are supposed to forgive, in reality, the majority of us struggle with it; especially if the person who has hurt you has not shown any remorse or regret for what they have done. However, regardless of how difficult it may be, extending forgiveness is something we must do because God requires it. Besides, if we are going to be in line with the will of God, we have to be obedient to all of His word—not just the parts we like.

Moreover, when God instructs us to forgive it is because He knows it is in our own best interest to forgive. Whether you understand it or not, victims are the ones who receive the most benefit from forgiveness. When you forgive you are helping yourself not the other person. For example, forgiving someone releases you from the anger and bitterness that comes with being hurt. It also allows you to receive the healing, peace and blessings that come with being in line with God's will. In addition, it spares you from the consequences of living life with an unforgiving heart. Years ago, I heard a preacher say, "Forgiveness is your personal pathway to peace. If you want peace in your life after being hurt, start by forgiving those who did you wrong."

When we talk about extending forgiveness to the individual(s) who have hurt us, I am cognizant it is easier for some than it is for others. There are some people who can easily let it go and move on like nothing ever happened. One the other hand, there are those who just cannot seem to let it go or get beyond what happened. Whether you struggle with extending forgiveness or not, it can be a challenge when you have to keep forgiving the same person. It is hard enough forgiving an individual for one incident, but it's even harder when you have to forgive the same person numerous times.

If I can be transparent for a moment, I want you to know that I love God and try my best to be a good Christian; but, I have moments when I struggle with forgiving the same person over and over. Yes, I'm growing spiritually and I am trying to do everything God requires in his word. Still, I have a hard time forgiving someone who constantly does harmful and evil things to me. I know that as a believer I am supposed to forgive. I also know regardless of how many times that person does me wrong I should keep forgiving him or her. However, I do not always feel like doing the right thing. There are times when instead of forgiving them, I wanted to lay hands on them. For the record, when I say lay hands, I'm not talking about praying. Please do not judge me for being transparent, just keep me lifted up in your prayers.

Even as a pastor, forgiving somebody who has hurt you and continues to do mean things to you is not an easy thing to do. It takes a whole lot of prayer and the power of the Holy Spirit to keep forgiving the same person. Regardless of how hard it is, we still have to do it because God requires it in His Word. Therefore, if God said it, that settles it and it must be done. When you are a child of God extending forgiveness has no limits.

This point of unlimited forgiveness is clearly made in Matthew, Chapter 18. Let's examine the context of the story so you will better understand the content. The Bible says Jesus was having a discourse with his disciples, teaching them what they should do when a brother or fellow believer sins against them. Jesus said in v. 15, if your brother sins against you the first thing you should do is go to him and show him his fault. Wow, I like that! The point Jesus is making is if someone offends you, the best way to address it is to go to that person and try to resolve it between the two of you.

Now, I found it quite interesting that Jesus did not say, when you have a problem with someone the first thing you should do is take it to the pastor or the deacons. He did not instruct them to go on social media and air out all their business. No, instead Jesus directs them to go to the person you have an issue with and try to resolve it between the two of you. Can you imagine how many issues would be resolved in church and in life if people would just go to each other and resolve their differences amongst themselves? Can you imagine how much drama would be eliminated in places of worship if people would just get together and talk about their issues instead of involving so many other people in their issues? Jesus says, if you have a problem with another person the first thing you should do is go to that person and try to resolve it together. The fewer people involved in your situation the better. It has been proven that the more people involved the more opinions and attitudes you have to deal with.

But if that does not work, then Jesus recommends you involve others. He urges taking one or two people with you to mediate and resolve the issue. If you still do not get anything accomplished, then take it to the church. Jesus is not telling them to take it to the church just so they can reveal and talk about the problem. He's instructing them to take it to the church so that the church can help resolve the problem. That has been a problem for many people. Instead of people in the church helping to solve the problem, they elevate or create even more problems. This is why we have to be careful to whom we take our problems and issues. Everybody in church is not qualified to solve or even help you with your problems. Please do not be confused, a person who has a title or a high position is not always spiritually qualified to help you work through your issues with another person.

If you cannot resolve it amongst yourself, take it to the church. If the church cannot help, or if the other person does not want to listen to the advice of the church; then He says, treat that person as you would a pagan or tax collector. Distance yourself from that person because it is obvious he or she does not want a solution to the problem. Unfortunately, not everyone who has a problem is willing to sit down with you and resolve it. Some people like to keep problems present. Even in our churches, everybody who has an issue with another individual is not always willing to sit down to come up with some sort of solution. Instead of resolving the issue, they get other people involved and it eventually becomes a distraction for the entire church. But this is totally contrary to how Jesus instructs us to handle disputes and disagreements with other people, especially brothers and sisters in Christ.

After Jesus taught them about how to handle disputes with others, Peter came to Jesus and said, Lord I remember you said that we are to forgive those who sin against us. The question I have is how many times do we have to forgive them? How many times do we have to let it go? Then Peter asks, up to seven times? Peter thought he was doing something great when he suggested, seven times. He said, Lord I think seven times is more than fair, since the rabbis and the Jewish custom only require that you forgive a person three times. But Jesus said, No Peter, not just seven times, but seventy times seven.

Peter thought he was being generous by offering to forgive a person seven times. Jesus, however, wanted Peter and the other disciples to know that the amount of times you extend forgiveness does not have a numerical limit. He says Peter, as a child of God you must keep on forgiving, because extending forgiveness should be limitless. Jesus says it does not matter how many times a person sins against you, as one of His followers we have to keep on forgiving. Irrespective of how many times a person hurts you, betrays you, lies on you, switches up on you, talks bad about you and does evil things to you, as a believer you have to keep on forgiving.

Perhaps, you may be muttering to yourself this is beyond my pay grade. Yet, it's what God requires from us as believers and followers of Christ. Another reason why we must continually forgive others is because God continually forgives us. If you have never made a mistake or done anything wrong against God or anyone else, then you can hold a grudge as long as you want. If you are perfect and have never sinned, you too can stay angry for the rest of your life. But if you have messed up at least one time and have done at least one thing wrong to someone else, God had to forgive you. Since our Heavenly Father forgave you, you must do the same for others. I can hear you saying, but I already forgave that person and they just keep doing stuff. I let the last thing go and they turned around and did something else. God says so did you. If we are honest with ourselves, God forgave and continues to forgive us for the all the things we do. Even after being forgiven, we messed up again. In reality, we are no better than the people who keep offending us. Why? Because we keep offending God and needing forgiveness.

If forgiving a person repeatedly is something you refuse to do, that is your personal choice. Just keep this in mind, if we do not extend forgiveness, we will not receive it. Remember what Jesus says in Matthew 6:15, "If you do not forgive men their sins, your Father will not forgive your sins." If we do not forgive and let go of what someone did to us, God will not forgive and let go of the all the stuff we did to Him. It also means that God is going to treat us the same way we treat others. Therefore, the best thing for us to do, regardless of how you feel, is to forgive and keep on forgiving.

Let's face it, there is a difference between letting things go and putting it aside. A lot of people get the two confused especially as it relates to forgiveness. When you forgive and really forgive, you let it go. When you have not really forgiven, you just put it aside until that person makes you angry again. When they make you angry or do something you do not like, you pick it back up and throw it in their face. Unfortunately, that's not forgiveness. You cannot move on until you have truly extended forgiveness.

For some reason many people think that because they put it aside, they have moved on. That is far from the truth. When a person really moves on, they no longer allow what someone did to them to influence their current emotions, thoughts, or behaviors. If you still get angry when you see the person(s) who hurt you and you still have the urge to get even, that means you have not truly forgiven and you have not moved on. When you can be in the presence of the person who hurt you and it does not disturb your peace or distract you from what you were doing, it's a sign that you have moved on. True forgiveness is when you can get the person and what they have done to you completely out of your mind. You are no longer bothered by the thought of them. This is the place where we all have to get to in life, a place of total forgiveness.

Don't Be Like the Unmerciful Servant

One of the worst things we can do as believers is receive God's grace and mercy, but not extend it to others. For instance, we receive God's forgiveness for all the things we did wrong, but we refuse to forgive others for their offenses against us. We get another chance, but we do not give others another chance. Unfortunately, this happens in many of our churches. People who have been forgiven and delivered from their issues will judge and hold people captive who have issues. Some people in church will not let you forget about your issues. They constantly ridicule you because of the things you did wrong. What's amazing is some of those same individuals wanted the church to forgive them when they used bad judgment; yet, they refuse to forgive another person who has errored in their ways. I heard a preacher say, "People in the church don't believe in extending grace and forgiveness until they need it." When we do that, we become just like the unmerciful servant in Matthew, Chapter 18 who refused to extend the same grace he was given.

The Parable of the Unmerciful Servant (Matthew 18: 21-35)

21 Then Peter came to Jesus and asked, "Lord, how many times shall I forgive my brother or sister who sins against me? Up to seven times?" 22 Jesus answered, "I tell you, not seven times, but seventy-seven times. 23 "Therefore, the kingdom of heaven is like a king who wanted to settle accounts with his servants. 24 As he began the settlement, a man who owed him ten thousand bags of gold[b] was brought to him. 25 Since he was not able to pay, the master ordered that he and his wife and his children and all that he had be sold to repay the debt. 26 "At this the servant fell on his knees before him. 'Be patient with me,' he begged, 'and I will pay back everything.' 27 The servant's master took pity on him, canceled the debt and let him go. 28 "But when that servant went out, he found one of his fellow servants who owed him a hundred silver coins. He grabbed him and began to choke him. 'Pay back what you owe me!' he demanded. 29 "His fellow servant fell to his knees and begged him, 'Be patient with me, and I will pay it back.' 30 "But he refused. Instead, he went off and had the man thrown into prison until he could pay the debt. 31 When the other servants saw what had happened, they were outraged and went and told their master everything that had happened. 32 "Then the master called the servant in. 'You wicked servant,' he said, 'I canceled all that debt of yours because you begged me to. 33 Shouldn't you have had mercy on your fellow servant just as I had on you?' 34 In anger his master handed him over to the jailers to be tortured, until he should pay back all he owed. 35 "This is how my heavenly Father will treat each of you unless you forgive your brother or sister from your heart."

Here is the lesson that this story teaches us: When a believer comes to know God and receives grace for the immense debt of sin we have accrued against our Creator, we can no longer hold the sins of others against them. To do so would be like a slap in the face of God who forgave us. It will also show that we do not love Him enough to forgive others— when He invites all to be forgiven in Christ. If our faith is genuine, and our hearts are right with God, we should be like Him and extend unlimited forgiveness. If a person has hurt you and done some evil things to you, forgive them and keep on forgiving them just like God is doing for all of us. The bottom line is this; Christians ought to be the most forgiving people on earth because they have been forgiven as no one else has.

This parable also teaches us there is a penalty for not forgiving and showing mercy. In v. 35, the master handed the unforgiving servant over to the jailers to be tortured until he paid back what he owed. Although this was a parable, it should serve as a warning to all believers. Namely: Christians who have received mercy, but fail to show mercy to others will be subject to divine chastisement and consequences. Therefore, I challenge you to forgive and keep on forgiving so that you will not be like the unmerciful servant.

Discussion Questions:

1. How many times should we forgive the same person?

2. What happens if we do not forgive others?

3. What if a person never says sorry, do we still have to forgive them?

4. If a person is struggling with forgiving someone, how can we help them?

Chapter Eleven

The Charge

Chapter Eleven

The Charge

"Forget the former things; do not dwell on the past. See, I am doing a new thing! Now it springs up; do you not perceive it? I am making a way in the wilderness and streams in the wasteland."
Isaiah 43:18-19

IN THE BEGINNING of this book I talked about "church hurt" and how it has caused many people to leave the church and never return. Some people have even given up on God because of what they went through at church. I also talked about the misunderstanding of the word "church hurt." Most of the times when people say they have been hurt by the church, they are really referring to being hurt by someone in the church. For instance, if they had a disagreement with the pastor, or another member lied or mistreated them, they often call that "church hurt." When situations like this happen, the person who has been hurt may stop giving and stop supporting the activities in the church. They are angry, but they continue to show up for Sunday service; not for worship, just to get a point across and show their displeasure with those who offended them. Sometimes, they may just leave the church altogether.

When people leave their church because of "church hurt," they usually have something negative to say to others about the church. In my opinion, this is unfair because it was not the entire church that hurt them. It was an individual

169

who was a part of the church. Therefore, a negative label should not be placed on the entire church because of something that happened with a particular person. I am not minimizing anyone's experience nor am I suggesting that churches do not have issues. With that in mind, I do not believe churches are bad places. There are just people with bad attitudes and proclivities in our churches. Yet, I'm crazy enough to believe there are many good people in every church. This why I always say, the entire church should not suffer because of the actions of a few.

One of the reasons I wrote this book is because I do not want anyone who has had a bad experience at church to give up on the church or God. I believe the church is important in all of our lives and in the lives of our families. Anything that can push us away from church and cause us to walk away from God is a victory for the devil. So, I want to challenge you to stick with God and stay connected to a church. Do not allow anything or anybody to push you away.

If you have been hurt in church, by the pastor, a leader, or by another member, now is the time to forgive them and release the anger from your heart. Remember when you forgive you are not validating what they did to you, neither are you telling the person what they did is ok. When you forgive you are just giving a blessing of peace to yourself. What many people do not understand is that forgiving a person does not mean you have to like the person. Neither does it mean you have to be friends with the person. You can for-give a person and never say a word to them.

As I stated before, forgiveness is not about the person who hurt you, but rather all about you. Forgiveness is a form of liberation. It actually sets you free from the person and what they did to you. It also empowers you to move on with your life. Even if they doing evil things to you, keep forgiving them so that you can will peace of mind. You owe it to your-self. If you have forgiven the person who hurt you, but for some reason you still cannot find any peace, it may be time for you to find another church. By no means am I trying to encourage you to just up and leave your church. I would, however, rather you find another church than sit in your current church angry and distracted from worship; that's self-inflicted pain. Speaking for myself, I would not sit in a church where I cannot enjoy the service or the fellowship because of a previous problem. At some point you have to do what's best for your soul and your peace of mind.

Here's my charge to you: whether you were hurt at church or by people from the church, it's time to do yourself a favor (if you have not already done so) and move on. Let God handle it. It is my prayer that you will not allow what happened to you at church to keep you from going to church or hinder your worship when you get there. What someone did to you may have caused some major problems and pain in your life, but you survived and you are a stronger person now than you were before. Walk in your victory and let the devil know that he may have knocked you down, but he could not keep you down. Close the door on your past and enjoy your future. Please do not allow the pain you experienced at church, cause you to hate the church. Whatever you do, please do not give up on God or the church!

Practical Steps to Overcome and Heal from Church Hurt

1. **Don't blame God for the actions of people.**
   Remember it was not God who hurt you, it was His people. Church attendance does not suggest that people won't be cruel and ungodly. No one in church is perfect, even those with titles and positions fall short of the glory of God.

2. **Pray and keep on praying**.

   Pray that God will help you heal and forgive so that you can have peace and move on with your life. The Bible says in Mark 11:25, "Whenever you stand praying, forgive, if you have anything against anyone, so that your Father who is in heaven will also forgive you your transgressions."

3. **Stick with God and His Church.**

   When a person experiences "church hurt" one of the first things they do is leave the church and join another. But one thing we must all keep in mind is, there is no perfect church. As long as the church has people on the inside, it will never be perfect. Every church has problems and people who will make you angry, lie on you, and do some evil things to you; it's just a fact that we all have to face. Although the people in the church are not perfect, we serve a perfect God who can help you in all situations. Therefore, never allow people to push you away from God or fellowship with the saints.

4. **Forgive and keep on forgiving until you are able to and move on.**

I know it's hard, but, like it or not, we have to forgive. God said it, so let it be! Remember, forgiveness lifts the weight off of you and gives the burden to the Lord. You are not doing it for the person who hurt you, you are doing it for yourself. You owe that to yourself!

Bibliography

Articles

Alexander, Paul, *What To Do When You Disagree With Your Pastor*, 2018.

Lawless, Chuck, *12 Reasons Why People Leave A Local Church*, 2018.

Piper, Barnabas, *Dear Future Pastor, A Letter Teaching Them What PK's Would Like Them To Know*, 2016.

Piper, Barnabas, *3 Things Pastor's Kids Need From Churches*, 2017.

Powell, Frank, *12 Sings You Are A Modern Day Pharisee*, 2017.

Stumbo, Ellen, Confessions of a Pastor's Wife: When I Don't Like Church, 2013.

Books

Corprew-Boyd, Dr. Angela, Church Hurt: The Wounded Trying To Heal, Creation House, Lake Mary, FL, 2008.

Lotz Graham, Anne, *Wounded by God's People*, Zondervan, Grand Rapids, MI, 2013.

Mansfield, Stephen, *Healing Your Church Hurt: What to do when you still love God but you have been wounded by his people*, Barna, Austin, Texas, 2012.

Stetzer, ED; Dobson, Mike, *Comeback Churches*. B & H Publishing, Nashville, TN, 2007.

Thompson, M. Nina, *Church Hurt Ain't No Joke*, Rycraw Productions, St. Louis Missouri, 2011.

Williams, Dr. Jamie, *Ouch! I Got Church Hurt: A Guide to Turning Your Pain into Purpose*, Life Impacting Ministries, Inc., Peachtree City, GA, 2017.

ABOUT THE AUTHOR

Dr. Vernon D. Shelton, Sr. is a native of Baltimore, MD. He attended Coppin State University where he earned a Bachelor of Science in Criminal Justice. An avid athlete, Shelton played for Coppin's baseball team under former Orioles center fielder Paul Blair; and eventually, he went on to play semi-pro baseball in the state of Maryland. Dr. Shelton earned a Master's of Divinity degree at The Samuel Dewitt Proctor School of Theology at Virginia Union University Seminary. In June of 2012 Dr. Shelton earned his Doctorate of Ministry degree from the United Theological Seminary, in Dayton Ohio.

He received and accepted the call to the preaching ministry on March 1, 2002 at Jerusalem Baptist Church under the leadership of Pastor Mamie Cooley. He later served as Youth Pastor at the New Bethlehem Baptist Church under the leadership of Dr. Anthony M. Chandler, Sr. Four years later he was called to pastor his first church, The New Hope Christian Baptist Church in Baltimore, Maryland. He served as the senior pastor of New Hope from 2006 to 2010. On September 19, 2010 Dr. Shelton was installed as the tenth pastor of the Holy Trinity Baptist Church in Amityville, NY. During the first year of Dr. Shelton's arrival, Holy Trinity experienced significant growth, spiritually and numerically. God has blessed Holy Trinity under Dr. Shelton's leadership to add an 8am morning worship service. In just eight years of pastoring Holy Trinity. Dr. Shelton has led the congregation in numerous Capital Campaigns; which they successfully raised money to complete major renovations to the sanctuary and fellowship hall, install a new parking lot and renovate the church annex.

Dr. Shelton has authored two other books entitled, "Picking Up The Pieces" and "Changing The Way We Do Church." He serves as the President of Eastern Baptist Association Congress of Christian Education. In addition, he also serves as the area Vice-President for the Empire State Convention Congress of Christian Education. Dr. Shelton serves as a writer for the National Baptist Congress of Christian Education Study Guide. He is a federally certified Chaplain, and very active in the community. In September 2017, Dr. Shelton founded the Developing Disciples Empowerment Institute, an accredited Bible College located in Long Island, NY. He is a firm believer that every aspect of life and ministry should be done in excellence. His favorite motto is *"excellence is not the standard, but the minimum."* He is a devoted husband to his wife, LaPrena, and the proud father of Terrance, Monique, Myriah *(stepdaughter)*, Ayona, and Vernon, Jr and is delighted by the family's newest addition, his grandson, Amari.

"The Spirit of the Lord is on me, because He has anointed me to preach good news to the poor. He has sent me to proclaim freedom for the prisoners and recovery of sight for the blind, to release the oppressed, to proclaim the year of the Lord's favor."
Luke 4:18-19

Additional Books Written By

Dr. Shelton

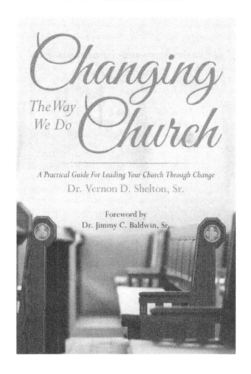

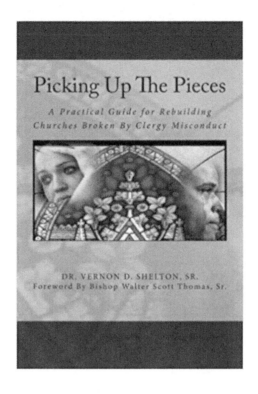

.

11323059R00105

Made in the USA
Monee, IL
09 September 2019